H17782

THE
BEST YEARS
OF YOUR LIFE

THE
BEST YEARS
OF YOUR LIFE

PLANNING THE PERFECT RETIREMENT

Alexander and Margaret Bowie

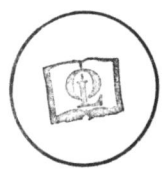

BLANDFORD PRESS
POOLE · NEW YORK · SYDNEY

First published in the UK 1986 by Blandford Press
Link House, West Street, Poole, Dorset, BH15 1LL

Copyright © 1986 Margaret & Alexander Bowie

Distributed in Australia by
Capricorn Link (Australia) Pty Ltd,
PO Box 665, Lane Cove, NSW 2066

British Library Cataloguing in Publication Data

Bowie, Alexander
    The best years of your life : planning
    the perfect retirement.
    1. Retirement
    I. Title   II. Bowie Margaret
    646.7'9   HQ1062

ISBN 0 7137 1713 0

Typeset by Lovell Baines Print Ltd, Hollington Farm, Woolton Hill,
Newbury, Berkshire.

Printed in Great Britain by Biddles Ltd, Guildford

CONTENTS

ACKNOWLEDGEMENTS

Our thanks are due to all those whose suggestions and encouragement have helped in preparation of this book. In particular, we thank the Metropolitan Police for hints on security inside and outside the home; James Shortt, international military advisor specialising in close quarter battle, for advice on self-defence; the Army School of Catering at Aldershot for tips on a balanced diet for pensioners, and on eating for warmth; and Roz-Eddie's Gym, who planned a series of get-fit exercises for the over fifties. For expert advice on money management we turned to Robin Dunham FCA, ASIA, who contributed Chapter 3 and Paul W. Greeley FCA, ATII, who provided the latest information on the State earnings-related pension scheme (SERPS). We would also thank the Editor of *Choice*, and Glenn Barker, for permission to reproduce material concerning Mr and Mrs Judd's garden which received a *Garden News* award, and the Editor of *Your Retirement* and Judith Carter, for permission to include details of Mr and Mrs Lofthouse's garden which received an award from *Garden Answers*. We are also grateful to all those who co-operated in the chapter on case histories, and to our relatives and friends who provided a great deal of useful information.

Margaret and Alexander Bowie
London, 1986

INTRODUCTION

This book is intended for the man or woman who has not yet retired, who is still active and in reasonable health. The thrust is towards people in their 50s, those who know that in a few years' time they will have to change their lifestyle, either by taking early retirement or by adapting to a different way of living so as to avoid a tremendous upheaval at the age of 60 or 65.

Some of the suggestions in the book may seem more relevant to older age groups but, if you are going to spend money on making necessary changes, it is a shrewd move to plan for this now and not to wait until you have less energy and less cash.

When we talk about 'planning' we do not mean rigid, hard and fast schemes. Anyone who has been around for 50 odd years knows that in life there is no such thing as a fixed plan – there are only options. You may decide on one route, but the Almighty, or circumstances, can steer you onto another. You need to be sufficiently adaptable to make contingency arrangements to meet this.

All this adds up to survival. One definition of surviving is 'to continue to exist in spite of'. What we have set out to do is not only to help you to exist in spite of retirement but to enjoy it, to keep your health and looks, to give to as well get from the community, to work – if you want to – and to do it all in your own way.

Practically everything applies equally whether you are Mr, Mrs or Ms, married or single, widowed or divorced. Retirement is a change of course. It is a challenge to you as to how you spend what could well be another two decades.

There has been too much talk about the 'problems' of retirement. We do not know why this phase of life has been singled out as an exceptionally difficult time. Whoever puts great emphasis on the 'problems' of getting married, of buying your first home, of starting a family? Retirement should be approached in the same positive way, as something to be looked forward to and enjoyed.

In an ideal society there would be no compulsory retirement date. People age at completely different rates and should be able to work as long as they wish. If we cannot achieve that, then at least retirement should be a flexible matter, with some finishing early and others going on well into their 70s.

The demand for flexibility is strong in a number of countries, particularly Canada and Switzerland. In France, retirement is regarded as one of the four phases of life – learning, earning, retirement and dependence, whereas in Britain the last two phases seem to be lumped together in the minds of governments of all colours, and in the minds of the trade unions who concentrate their efforts on earlier and earlier compulsory retirement dates. Between them all, they are likely to build one of the biggest human scrap-heaps in the world.

What is needed is more awareness of the need for preparation for the third phase, that of changing from full-time to part-time employment or to self-employment of a paid or voluntary nature. There should be far greater provision for the retraining of those who want to go on earning so that, while people in their 20s are moving up the promotion ladder, those in their 40s are getting ready for a change of role. There are existing facilities which go some of the way to meeting this need – the Open University courses and the Government vocational training schemes – but these need to be considerably expanded.

Professor Charles Handy of the London Business School was recently quoted in *The Times* as saying that paid employment was likely to become simply one phase of life. Taking the view of the French, that retirement is the third and not the final phase, he said: 'Organisations are becoming more like the armed services, taking people for twenty years, not for ever. So you need to prepare for life beyond retirement'.

Engineers' professional institutions have been aware of this for some time and have urged their members to take courses in management studies to supplement their technical qualifications. This is to equip them not only to take over divisions within large organisations, but to be able to grasp the roles of sales, accounts, promotion and industrial relations, as well as their own speciality so that when redeployment arises, these trained all-rounders will be fitted to run their own companies.

But although the 'out at 40' approach is increasing, very many people still remain in their jobs until the official retirement date. Pre-retirement courses are run by specialist groups or by local authorities and, in other instances, by banks, insurance companies or large firms. These excellent courses are generally geared to the age of 60, some taking place later when retirement at 65 is only a year away. Recently, however, there has been a growing realisation that even this form of more immediate planning for retirement should start earlier, while people are still in their 50s. In this way, the abrupt change from employment to retirement could be avoided.

What is not always appreciated is that there is no sharp cut-off between the roles that people play during their lives. The man of 50 who has had to take early retirement may have already become a grandfather, but he may also have elderly parents about whom he is concerned. He may still be paying off a mortgage and, at the same time, be contributing to the further education of his younger children. So it is too much of a generalisation to talk about the retired as if they are a homogeneous mass, utterly alike, totally indistinguishable from each other.

Like every other group of society, the retired group is composed of widely differing individuals. Their response to retirement will vary from panic to elation. Their ability to make the right decisions over the next few years will be linked directly to the amount of thought they have given to retirement. To help you make the right decisions in your own case we have tried to sort out some of the maze. Much will depend on two key factors – health and money – and these will be the subject of the first chapters.

1 HEALTH, EXERCISE AND MORALE

Shortly before you retire, arrange for a check-up with your doctor. Health is the most important asset you have and, if any change in lifestyle is necessary, then the sooner you make it the better. It may be less or different food, more exercise or the avoidance of stress. Someone living at home can be subject to stress as much as another person engaged in the rat-race; it is just that the stresses arise from other causes, one particularly common one being boredom.

It is a good opportunity at your check-up to ask about exercise or about taking up a sport. But remember, if you are out of condition, you have to get fit to start a sport, not use sport as a means of getting fit.

POSTURE

How well do you sit or stand? Take a look at yourself in the glass. If you slump or droop, you are being unkind to your spine, Without looking like an old-time recruitment poster, you need to have your head up, shoulders back and stomach tucked in, whenever you are standing, sitting or walking. And, as always, you need to breathe in and out rhythmically. When sitting, keep your rear against the back of the chair and sit so that you feel the support of the chair back across your spine. It is better to cross your ankles than to cross your legs at the knee.

Very many of the common aches and pains result from poor posture – slumping in a chair, eating in a semi-crouched position bent over the plate, walking like an elderly penguin with shoulders bent forward and eyes on the ground. It is amazing how much better people feel when they stand well, sit up straight and walk as if they enjoyed it. None of these things will do you any harm, however much out of condition you have become.

Picking up something from the floor is a frequent source of backaches. Many people bend over, keeping their knees rigid, and put all the strain on their back muscles. Others know that you are supposed to bend at the knees, but they do not follow this through by keeping the head and shoulders up and letting the legs do all the work. If you visualise someone doing a formal curtsey, in a half-kneeling position with one foot slightly back, and looking up at the person to whom they are curtseying, you will get the right idea.

FEET

Many people suffer foot discomfort by the time they reach retirement age, although a good number of women will have done so for quite a while before then. To get the best out of your feet, try to find a shop which has fitters instead of a self-service arrangement and pay as much as you can afford for the shoes. Make use of the services of a chiropodist. Self-treatment is all right for the occasional corn, but real discomfort will not give way to amateur methods. The money spent will be well worthwhile in looking and feeling good. If your feet are comfortable you will be ready to take more exercise – if they are not, then you will head for the nearest chair. No form of exercise is any good and no sport is enjoyable if you are dragging around two aching feet. Baths and showers help to make them more comfortable, but a number of foot problems crop up in middle life because foot, ankle and leg muscles have taken a lot of punishment over the years from badly-fitting and poorly-designed shoes.

The converse can also apply on retirement. There is a tendency for some people to go to the other extreme and spend all day in slippers. Although that is more comfortable than wearing shoes which do not fit, slippers do not provide any real support and, if worn all the time, psychologically are a sign of giving up and growing old too quickly.

Although today it is harder to find shoes which really fit, there are still quite a few ranges which cater for people whose feet have spread or have a tendency to swell, or whose arches are not as strong as they were. If you can afford it, having found a place that sells comfortable shoes, buy two pairs rather than one. Shoes last longer if worn alternate days.

Economise on other things, but not on shoes. Neglected feet can upset muscles in other parts of the body as the sufferer alters his gait to avoid putting pressure on painful spots. Walking on the outside or inside of the foot causes pains up the outside of the leg and also affects the hip joint.

When it comes to heavy-duty footwear for icy weather, buy wellingtons one size larger so as to allow for a heavy pair of socks inside. Or go for the eskimo-type boot, light to wear and giving a strong grip on icy pavements. One drawback of wellingtons, if you live alone, is getting them on and off. There are extra-strong shoe-horns which can be useful, or boot-jacks of the type popular with hunting people. Suede or leather boots are more practical if there are two zip fasteners instead of one.

TAKING UP EXERCISE

As you get older, muscular strength gradually starts to reduce in most cases, but you can still go in for a wide variety of moderate exercise. In fact, it is an absolute necessity. Walking is free and swimming costs only a small amount, or nothing at all if your home is at the seaside.

Many doctors query the wisdom of taking up violent exercise after a largely sedentary life where total exertion may have consisted in getting in and out of the car or moving your armchair nearer the television set. If at 40 or 50 you have ambitions to be a squash champion, the fastest jogger in town or queen of the aerobics class, at least get medical clearance first. If not, you could be the fastest to arrive at the cemetery gates – feet first. So remember: go in for any sport very slowly and stop if it becomes a strain.

There will always be the exceptions who break all the rules by starting hang-gliding or parachuting at 70, but, for most people coming up to retirement, something less demanding is recommended. Among sports suggested by the Physical Education Association are walking, cycling and swimming. Tennis and badminton are also safe choices, provided that you ease into them and do not play with someone who is a lot better than you are so that you are constantly playing at your maximum. Golf is often recommended, but even that should be taken easily at first. A number of riding stables will supply suitable mounts and instruction for the late-starter. If you go jogging, start off by walking quickly and then jog for only a few minutes, gradually working it up. You will need well-fitting training shoes with adequate ankle protection. 'Jogger's ankle' is quite common and is not helped by badly-maintained and ill-lit pavements. Bowls used to be considered an old man's game but has now become popular with young and middle-aged men, and women too. If you decide to take up ski-ing, do not wait until your holiday starts. You will need special keep-fit classes to get you ready for this sport and at least the basic instruction at one of the dry-slopes where training is given. If you have been ski-ing for years, there is not the slightest reason why you cannot go on doing it when you are well past 40, but, if you are taking it up for the first time, there is the problem that a broken leg takes longer to knit the older you get, and you can run into arthritic problems later on.

One final word of advice: if indulging in any energetic sport, never go straight into a cold shower immediately afterwards, Wind down by a stroll around for a while and then go for a tepid shower rather than an icy cold one.

EXERCISE ROUTINES

Most people benefit from regular exercise but there are a minority who do not, so be on the alert if you feel any symptoms of dizziness or pain around the heart or breathing difficulties. These may only be signs that you need to exert yourself more, because you have not done so for too long, but they should always be checked out with your doctor and, even after you have seen him, if they occur while carrying out gentle exercise, it is advisable to stop and have a rest.

For the majority of people, the key word is 'moderation'. The best types of exercise are those which get rid of stiffness and make you more flexible. Many of these are the limbering-up type which professional dancers go in for before rehearsals. These include a whole range of bending and stretching movements – nothing exaggerated – reinforced by skipping and running on the spot. If you want to take it further than that, there are specific exercises to strengthen muscles of the stomach, legs and arms. A short course at a gym will lay the foundation for your daily dozen, after which you can go ahead on your own, allowing about 15 minutes a day and working up to double that time. If you have not exercised for quite a while, you will quickly notice the improvement: no more struggling up from that chair, or puffing when you bend down to pick up something.

The right way to set about exercising is by starting off with a series of simple movements of the type you were set at school to warm you up at the beginning of a PT session out of doors on a cold day. These are designed also to make you more supple so that, when you come to do rather more strenuous movements, you can do these more easily and without sudden jerks.

The most important exercise of all is breathing. Few people use their lungs to the fullest extent. Before starting any exercises, breathe in slowly, hold your breath and then let it out gently. Keep this up for about 5 minutes and then give your arms and legs something to do.

There are any number of arm exercises which do not involve moving from the spot. Most consist of swinging the arms around the body or over the head, stretching them out sideways then flinging them backwards as if you were swimming. When you have gone through these, you can continue the limbering up by bending towards each foot in turn.

For leg exercises the only equipment needed is a chair to provide something to hold on to while you swing each leg out sideways, then forwards and backwards. When you have mastered this routine, you can proceed to running on the spot, slowly at first, then faster, and finally back to the slower speed. A skipping rope is the only item needed for the next stage, which is best taken very gently at first before lifting your knees higher and skipping faster and then dropping the speed again.

None of these exercises should be prolonged. Allow 1 minute for each, increasing it to 3 or 4, with breathing exercises in between each group of exercises.

Even when you are sitting, there is scope for movement. Wriggle your toes, move one leg over the other from time to time, flex your fingers, shrug your shoulders occasionally. One well-known surgeon used to carry out a simple exercise when doing the round of the wards. Instead of planting his feet firmly on the ground, he used to shift the weight to the ball of the foot, rising on his toes, or sometimes letting the heel take the strain. Watch royalty, who often have to stand for hours and look as if they are enjoying it. They have worked out a knack of standing so as to vary the weight distribution.

One of the plus points about a basic exercise routine is that it costs nothing. There is no need for expensive equipment, such as stationary bicycles, exercise benches, pulleys or weights. Like walking, it all comes free in return for a small effort.

However, some people need the motivation of being with others when carrying out an exercise routine. In that case a weekly gym session is well worthwhile, provided that you carry on with the exercises on the other 6 days. A number of gymnasia now have workouts for retired people – men and women on separate days – and offer an exercise programme tailored to the needs of the more mature. So you need not feel self-conscious about a bulging tummy or slack muscles, as you are not likely to be surrounded by a crowd of bronzed Miss or Mr Universes.

Our local gym, Roz-Eddie in south London, provides training for the retired, with shower, plus sauna and massage if required. The timings of the sessions are usually in the quieter periods of the day rather than at busy evenings or weekends. Particular trouble spots can be tackled –

there are suitable exercises for tightening up tummy muscles, taking the creaks out of neck and shoulders, getting rid of 'dowager's hump' and, in the case of women who are otherwise in good condition, eliminating the flab that tends to accumulate on thighs and upper arms.

They say that, as people become middle-aged or older, they tend to have troubles arising from stiff joints. Their course of exercises to keep joints supple includes rotating the head while keeping a straight back, then, in turn, rotating the wrists, forearms and the whole arm from the shoulder down. Next comes rotation of the upper body, leaning forward and then backwards slightly while not moving the hips. Rotations of the knees and ankles come next, followed by gentle kicking to help the hip bones, and a final exercise where you bend over and bounce the upper part of the body to loosen up back and hamstrings, Their advice is: start with five or ten in each case, working up to twenty. Do everything at the same speed – it does not matter if it is slow to begin with as it will increase later.

Wherever you exercise, there is no need for elaborate or expensive clothing. A leotard with tights, boxer shorts and a tee shirt, or a very lightweight tracksuit, are all appropriate. The important thing is that the clothing should not distract from the exercising, which it would do if it were ill-fitting, too warm or too tight.

Having established a routine, either on your own or at a gym, it is essential to stick to it. A short session every day is far more beneficial than a much longer one only once a week.

DANCING

You can still keep in trim on dark winter evenings, when the weather is just not suitable for taking exercise out of doors. There is no age bar on dancing and some of the best dancers can be seen among the over 60s. This applies also to the more vigorous styles such as quick South American rhythms or country dancing.

APPEARANCE

A spin-off from going dancing is that it provides an incentive to dress up and look your best and, in the case of a woman, to have your hair done. Most hairdressers offer special rates in the early part of the week when staff are slack, which can show a big money-saving. Some also allow special rates in the case of OAPs. If you avoid the peak days of Friday and Saturday, you can have an inexpensive shampoo, set and trim. At one of our local hairdressing schools they include a free manicure while your hair is drying.

Some day centres provide hairdressing services, as they realise that there is nothing which boosts a woman's morale more than knowing that her hair looks its best.

Some years ago, wigs in all colours and styles were very popular, but the choice is now more limited. However, they can be handy for an occasion when you are asked out and there is no time to get to the hairdresser. Choose an easy-care style which can be dunked in the basin and left to dry overnight. Wigs which require professional dressing start off by being expensive and go on becoming more so because setting them is a slow and difficult job. When choosing a wig, go for a shade a little lighter than your normal hair colour, avoiding the harsh blacks and chilly whites. To blend in the wig with the skin tones of the face, eyes and eyebrows need to be subtly emphasised. Underdo it and you could resemble a rabbit; overdo it and you might be mistaken for Danny la Rue.

One hazard that some wives face as they grow older is that their husbands still like them to keep the hairstyle which they wore when they first met. One man we know hated any hair that was not at least shoulder-length and it took his wife a lot of tact and many months to persuade him that a swept-up or swept-back style made her look a lot younger.

Others are quite keen to see their wives keep up with fashion and, when they take this attitude, their advice is well worth seeking, however unpalatable. Sons and grandsons are also useful in this respect because, like husbands, they look at the whole picture and not, like many women, at the hairstyle divorced from its wearer. But never ask advice a few minutes before you set out for the evening. The frank comments could undermine your confidence completely!

When it comes to make-up, daughters and granddaughters are a better source of advice. You are no competition and they enjoy helping an older person to look their best, so you will get an honest appraisal and some kind help. Eye make-up is one of the pitfalls for the older woman. False eyelashes look ghastly, unless cropped so short that they blend in with your own. If mascara is used at all, it should be brown or grey rather than black. In any case, it often makes older eyes look more tired than they would in their natural state.

Talking to our local drama schools on the subject of retaining a youthful appearance when past middle age, they came up with several useful tips, based on the training given to a young actor or actress who had to play the part of an older person.

One summed it up by saying: 'It all comes to stiff joints and unused muscles. A young and supple person in good condition has to learn to keep the torso rigid, walking from the knees instead of from the hips, if playing an elderly role'.

Another said: 'The biggest give-away of joints and muscles that are not being properly used is when getting up from an armchair. For someone in good condition this should be a smooth one-piece action. For many older people it is a grunt-and-groan effort, with two or three attempts at rising before actually managing to get up'.

An actress who gets away with looking 50 when nearly 20 years older explained: 'Whenever I sit down, I put one foot behind the other and lower myself into the chair fairly slowly. As I rise, I place one hand palm downwards on the seat, which helps to lever myself up'. This is equally suitable for men and women, and makes sitting down and getting up more comfortable than plopping heavily into a chair, jarring stiff joints as you do it.

Asked about other give-away signs she told us: 'Don't fuss. Constantly opening and shutting a handbag in the case of a woman, or continually adjusting tie, shirt cuffs or the knees of trousers in the case of a man, are ageing signs, When we're young, we're all told not to fidget, but a lot of us slip back into the habit when we're older, when it's even more necessary to appear calm and poised'.

PHYSICAL ATTRIBUTES

When you are about to retire, take stock of your physical attributes. Natural teeth and dentures need regular servicing just as much when you are retired as when you were working. So do eyes and ears. If there is any tendency to be overweight, it is often easier to shed the necessary pounds while still working than when you are home more of the day and subject to nibbling between meals because of boredom.

Eyes

If you wear glasses you will need to continue to have your eyes checked at least every 2 or 3 years. As you get older you need more light, so it is advisable to check that there are no very dark spots in the home and that passages and stairways are brightly lit.

If the optician recommends bifocals, take time to get used to them before deciding that they are not for you. For most people there can be some slight difficulty at first if you do not watch your step when going downstairs. There are, of course, the variable-focus lenses which are equally suitable both for close work and for long-distance vision. These suit nine out of ten people, but our own optician does not recommend them if you work as a draughtsman or do a great deal of copy typing.

Remember that eyes tire more easily as you become older and, in most people, there is some deterioration of vision. A bright but not glaring light is necessary for reading, sewing or other close work. Do not put off changing lenses for too long as, apart from the frustration of seeing badly, you will be more prone to accidents. Rest your eyes from time to time, especially after a lot of reading or viewing television, and use an eye bath regularly. Salt water is a tonic for tired eyes, especially for older people whose eyes tend to water more in cold winds. If you or your partner reads in bed, look out for specially-designed lamps which shine well on the pages while the rest of the room is in darkness.

Ears
Few people are self-conscious about wearing glasses these days, but too many still hesitate to apply for a hearing aid, somehow connecting this with greybeards in their dotage. There is no reason for this, because modern cordless aids are completely unobtrusive as well as being extremely efficient. In any case, hearing begins to deteriorate in many people as early as 35, so it is not something associated only with the very old.

Before deciding that your hearing is deteriorating, and hurrying out to buy a proprietary model, first go to see your doctor. All that may be needed is to have one or both ears syringed, to get rid of the accumulated wax. Never have a go at this yourself. It should be done professionally, either by the general practitioner or by a nurse at the local health centre.

If you live within reach of central London you can arrange an interview with the Royal National Institute for the Deaf. The Institute also supply much useful advice, as well as a free booklet *Special Aids to Hearing*.

Poor hearing, like poor vision, can be remedied and it is a pity to rob yourself of pleasure in company because you have to miss what is being said or keep asking people to repeat themselves.

Even with a hearing aid there are some people who still have difficulty in communication. Modern plug-in telephones have the advantage that they can be taken up to the bedroom at night, which ensures that the bell can be heard and that there is no need to get out of of a warm bed to answer the telephone call. If required, an extra loud bell can be fitted and the handset modified to make listening easier.

SLEEP

The argument has raged for a long time as to whether older people need more or less sleep. Actually, this seems to be a completely individual thing. Some settle down to an uninterrupted 8 hours as soon as their heads touch the pillow, while others sleep in fits and starts, supplemented by a series of cat-naps during the day. On the whole, if you have been a poor sleeper when you were younger, you are not very likely to improve as you pass 50.

With quite a few older people, it is cold which causes poor sleep. As circulation is not so good, it is essential to see that the bedroom and the bed itself are sufficiently warm – not hot, as there is nothing more conducive to insomnia than tossing and turning in an overheated room. A duvet is often more popular than a load of blankets, because it is both light and warm, but if you prefer blankets then it pays to get the best that you can. The cellular type provide good insulation and so are a good choice for both winter and summer.

If you like to take a nap after lunch, remember to deduct it from your night's sleep, as you may find yourself too wide awake to go off to sleep or may wake up around dawn and be unable to get to sleep again. Contrary to traditional ideas, you sleep better with the window shut during winter and with the room and adjoining rooms, such as the bathroom, at much the same temperature.

Sleeplessness may be a matter of insufficient fresh air – not at night but during the day. The old saying about 'after supper walk a mile' has some truth in it and there is no doubt that after a long spell in the fresh air – not necessarily in the evening – you often seem to get a better night's sleep.

If you have built up a habit of sleeping intermittently over the years, pills are not likely to be much help. It is better to accept the fact and provide for it. A thermos containing a hot milk drink can be taken up to bed each night. Coffee and tea are not a good idea as both are mildly stimulating. There should be a reading lamp with an adequate-wattage bulb and a bolster or extra pillow to make sitting up more comfortable. A simple backrest is worth getting if you do a lot of reading

A radio can also be on the bedside table. If your wife or husband has no difficulty in sleeping, both the radio and reading lamp can be of the type not likely to interfere with their comfort. There are lamps which direct the light only on to the book – of the type used in aircraft – and lightweight earphones are quite comfortable for listening to the radio.

All the same, it is worth experimenting to see whether a change in daily routine may be a solution. If you have been used to a heavy meal in the evening, try having it at mid-day and a light snack at night to see if that aids sleep. If you have a convenient 'local', see if the popular habit of taking the dog there for a walk will relax you sufficiently so that you no longer need to plan for a sleepless night.

If you want to mark your retirement with something which will be appreciated for the rest of your days, high on the list would be an adjustable bed. These can be bought as singles or doubles, or as twins which can be joined together to form a king-size bed. The most luxurious have automatic controls and, in the case of the twins, these are independently worked, to suit each sleeper. Most of these beds are pricey, but not if weighed against sound sleep, comfort and improved health.

2 FOOD AND DIET

Some people put on weight soon after retiring. The reason is that they continue with the same intake of food but take less exercise. A few pounds on or off do not matter; most people lose or gain from time to time for no apparent reason. Go on comfort factors – a skirt that will not zip up unless you hold your breath or a trouser belt that has to be let out a notch are early warnings to have a look at your diet.

Often it is not the quantity of food consumed but the balance which is wrong. Everyone knows about the three basics: proteins, fats, carbohydrates. Proteins are found in meat, fish, eggs, cheese and also in nuts and pulses. Fats are supplied by dairy products, plus margarine and animal and vegetable fat. Carbohydrates are supplied by bread, cereals, pastas and other flour-based products, together with sugar and starchy vegetables.

It is the type of food rather than the quantity which counts. Too much fat and carbohydrate will make you put on weight, but forget the miseries who would insist on a no-butter no-sugar regime. Unless the doctor has put you on a specific diet for health reasons, e.g. a low-fat one, use common sense and disregard the diet faddists. There is a great deal of talk about over-eating but it is just as important to avoid under-eating. Plenty of men and women living alone do just that because they cannot be bothered to cook for themselves.

If your diet is properly balanced, it is not going to do any harm to have the occasional fancy gateau, dollop of sugar or fried sausages. If one listened to all the theorists there is hardly a recipe in the average cookery book which could be prepared, because one or other ingredient would be prohibited.

As a general basis, if you get into the habit of eating the foods in the first list given below, and cutting back on those in the second list, you will not go far wrong.

Have plenty of: green vegetables – broccoli, brussels sprouts, cabbage, calabrese, kale, spinach; other vegetables – asparagus, bean sprouts, carrots, corn, leeks, lettuce, parsnips, red and green peppers, green peas, turnips, plus chives, garlic and parsley; seeds and nuts – e.g. sunflower seeds, mixed nuts; fruits – all citrus fruits, apricots, black-currants, blackberries, melon, peaches, strawberries, rosehips (best eaten raw or cooked for a minimum time) and also dried figs, prunes, currants; whole grains – bran, oats, rice, wheat, wheatgerm; fish – all types, but very little smoked fish; offal – liver and kidney; unrefined cold-pressed vegetable cooking oils; eggs and milk.

Cut down on: sausages – including frankfurters; luncheon meats; bacon; butter and margarine; fresh and sour cream; cream cheese; mayonnaise; salt; coffee; sugar and saccharin, including soft drinks containing this; cake mixes; alcohol.

When cutting down on salt and sugar, this not only means taking less sugar in tea and coffee and not adding salt on the plate, but also looking at the labels of tinned goods which often contain both sugar and salt. Tinned peas contain both, so do some processed meats, and soups are frequently heavily salted. If you are a keen coffee-drinker, try to cut it down by half and buy the darker rather than the light- or medium-roasted beans.

There is plenty of variety in the list of the 'goodies' above to provide interesting and enjoyable meals. And remember, this is a recommendation to emphasise these foods in the diet, not to stick solely to them. If you do not enjoy your meals, they will not do you much good, so a small quantity of the 'baddies' is better than cutting them out completely.

Even simple meals can be more enjoyable if eaten in pleasant company. When retiring, fix a regular date with friends to have lunch at each other's homes once a week. Having someone else to cater for makes eating an event, which stimulates the gastric juices and increases the appetite.

The pop-in lunch clubs play a very useful role, providing nourishing and well-balanced meals for a reasonable sum. People living alone can enjoy company and it gives an opportunity for married couples to meet others who have recently retired. With a good mid-day meal you can get by with a simple supper and modest breakfast. The advantage in having the main meal at mid-day is that there is no heavy cooking and clearing up in the evenings, and it is better to have a light meal at that time because you are likely to relax afterwards rather than take much exercise.

PLANNING MEALS

Thinking ahead in order to save unnecessary shopping trips is something most people have got used to while still working. If you have a freezer, you can avoid shopping in bad weather yet always have a reserve of food in stock. If you are buying a new refrigerator and do not want to have a separate freezer, it pays to choose a fridge with a very roomy section for frozen foods.

Freezers also give the opportunity to cook in advance. It takes no longer to boil up rice for four dishes than for one. When cooled, the other three portions can be put in plastic bags or freezer boxes, ready for puddings or curries. Someone with a larger chest freezer is able to organise for months ahead, but when there is only a small household you need to be careful not to become a slave to the freezer. That is why, on the whole, we favour a small freezer which is a useful back-up, caters for emergencies, but does not supply all your needs, so that there is a reason to get exercise by walking to the shops for fresh fruit and vegetables in season. The odd corners of a freezer can be used for plastic bags or boxes containing chives, parsley sprigs or made-up portions of mint sauce.

When you are busy with do-it-yourself and do not want to bother with sitdown meals, there is nothing more appetising than sandwiches, especially if granary bread is used. These can be prepared and kept in the freezer overnight. As a change from buttering the bread, spread it with the appropriate meat dripping plus a taste of the sauce which accompanies the roast, e.g. cold lamb and mint sauce, roast beef and horseradish. Another appetising choice is a cold bacon sandwich with a thin spread of bacon fat on the bread and a slice or two of fresh tomato. If you have a large thermos for tea or coffee and a wide-mouthed one for hot soup, you can get on with your do-it-yourself and still be well fed.

It is sometimes suggested that feeding well must be expensive. While it is true that food occupies a high proportion of most people's budgets, not all the money is always spent wisely and you could pay less for better value. Now that you have more time, it is possible to compare prices and to look out for bargains. Cooking in a saucepan that is divided up into three saves money, and so does filling the oven up with half-a-dozen dishes instead of burning fuel for one only.

Discussing this with the experts at the Army School of Catering at Aldershot, one very practical suggestion was that retired people could organise some of their shopping to take advantage of the economies of scale. No couple on their own could eat their way through a large fresh cabbage, but split up among three or four households it would be a means of ensuring fresh green vegetables for all of them. Root vegetables could be bought in the same way. In cold weather, they say, it is essential that older people eat more foodstuffs which provide warmth. After all, a soldier on Arctic duty has his rations almost doubled and more warmth-giving foods supplied. For OAPs this means plenty of carbohydrates – potatoes, wholemeal bread, pastry, spaghetti and other pastas. Extra proteins can be obtained from pulses – lentils, beans – and from reasonably-priced meat and fish, e.g. shin of beef, scrag end of lamb and herrings. There is no harm in increasing your fat intake during the winter; fat is needed to keep you warm and you burn it up at a faster rate than a younger person.

They were glad to see that 'junk food', which is eaten by pensioners as much as by youngsters, is becoming more worth having. Instead of burgers which had only a nodding acquaintance with beef, there are more whole-beef types around and pizzas which used to get by with a smear of tomato sauce and a sliver of cheese are now more likely to have a worthwhile amount of filling.

If you increase the amount of carbohydrates in your diet you will need to increase fibre, but this can be catered for easily by eating wholewheat bread and by choosing a bran breakfast cereal.

They pointed out that some older people have difficulty in peeling root vegetables, especially if they have rheumatism in their hands. Peeling is not necessary, however, and more nutriment and flavour are retained if vegetables are just lightly washed and then put in the saucepan, peel and all.

RECOMMENDED RECIPES

From their experience in keeping fighting men fit and well fed, whatever the weather, the Army School of Catering provided us with the following recipes, all of which are ideally suited to pensioners. All recipes are for two people.

Grilled Herrings with Mustard Sauce
Herrings
1 large or 2 small herrings
½ oz flour
salt and pepper to taste
½ oz cooking oil or margarine

Method

1. Scale, gut and wash the herrings (the fishmonger will do this for you on request).
2. Season the fish with salt and pepper and dip into the flour. This will not only help to seal in all the flavour but will prevent the fish from sticking to the tray during cooking.
3. Place on a greased or oiled tray and brush over with oil or melted margarine.
4. Grill the fish for 4 or 5 minutes, depending on its size and thickness, turning once so that both sides cook evenly.

Mustard Sauce

½ oz margarine
½ oz flour
¼ pint milk
¼ onion
1 clove
¼ oz prepared English mustard
salt to taste

Method

1. Melt the margarine in a small saucepan. Add the flour and cook to a sandy texture without colouring. Allow to cool on the side of the stove.
2. Boil the milk and gradually add to the cooked flour, stirring continually over a low heat. If the milk is added a little at a time, no lumps will form.
3. When the sauce is smooth and all the milk has been added, add the onion; if the clove is stuck into the side of the onion before adding it becomes easier to remove from the sauce when cooked.
4. Cook for 30 minutes at a gentle simmer.
5. Remove onion and clove, add the prepared mustard and serve with the fish.

Note: The recipe for mustard sauce up to and including Stage 4 is for a basic white sauce. By substituting chopped parsley for mustard we create a parsley sauce; chopped egg added makes an egg sauce. With this basic sauce, the possibilities are endless. Ready-made packet white sauces can be utilised and, to some extent, may work out to be more convenient. This method of cooking fish can be used for any type of fish, e.g. mackerel. Flavours can be enhanced by the addition of chopped fennel or other herbs to the flour in which the fish is dipped prior to grilling.

Fried Herring in Oatmeal

2 herrings

1 oz oatmeal
salt and pepper to taste
1 oz cooking fat or oil
Method
1. Split the herrings and remove the backbone (or ask the fishmonger to do this for you).
2. Season well and coat with oatmeal, pressing lightly to make it adhere to the flesh.
3. Fry in shallow fat or oil to a light golden brown on both sides.

Fish and Potato Pie
8 oz white fish
white sauce (see recipe for Mustard Sauce above)
8 oz mashed fresh or instant potato
½ oz breadcrumbs
½ oz margarine
Method
1. Poach the fish in a little salted water and drain.
2. Flake the fish and bind with the white sauce; season to taste.
3. Half fill a small pie dish or casserole with the fish mixture and cover with mashed potato.
4. Sprinkle with breadcrumbs and brush on melted margarine and bake in the oven at 350°F (180°C, Gas Mark 4) until golden brown.
Note: Smoked haddock can be substituted for white fish. Also, the addition of herbs will alter the flavour of the dish. A pastry topping can be substituted for the mashed potato; puff pastry can be purchased ready-made and, still as good but cheaper, so can shortcrust pastry.

Russian Steaks
10 oz minced beef
¼ oz parsley
½ oz butter
1 egg
½ oz flour
½ oz breadcrumbs
oil for frying
Method
1. Beat together the beef, parsley and butter and shape into two large steaks.
2. Egg, flour and breadcrumb the steaks.
3. Fry them for approximately 3 minutes per side in hot oil.

Shepherd's Pie
6 oz minced lamb
3 oz diced onion
salt and pepper to taste
½ oz tomato puree
2 oz flour
1 pint of stock made from a stock cube
8 oz mashed fresh or instant potato
½ oz margarine
Method
1. Fry the onion and mince
2. Add the seasoning, tomato puree and flour until a paste is formed and cook for 2 or 3 minutes.
3. Gradually add the stock and cook for 30 minutes.
4. Place in an ovenproof container.
5. Cover with the potato and neatly mark the top.
6. Brush with melted margarine and brown in a hot oven.

BASIC RATIONS

There comes a time when you are stuck at home and cannot get out to the shops. It might be a sudden snowfall, or you may have an invalid to look after and must wait in for the district nurse, or gas or electrical contractors may be due to arrive. To gear up for such emergencies, work out which of the items in your larder are necessary to keep you going for 2 or 3 days without having to go to the shops. Everyone's list will vary, according to eating habits, but here is one prepared by a couple who can boast that they have never run out of anything, however bad the weather.

In the freezer: a spare loaf or two, or some frozen dough; frozen green vegetables and orange juice for Vitamin C; frozen onion rings – it is surprising how many recipes need onions; a stewpack of mixed vegetables, for a wide range of casseroles; parsley, mint, chives – picked when young and fresh and frozen in small plastic bags; lamb's liver; streaky bacon; frozen apple rings, blackberries and other berry fruits.

In the fridge: butter, margarine, cheese, natural yoghurt, beef dripping.

In the larder: porridge or muesli; plain flour; dried yeast; evaporated, condensed and dried skimmed milk; Bovril; bottled lemon juice; instant dried potatoes and tinned potatoes; tea and coffee; honey; cooking oil; rice; stock cubes; sardines; dried and tinned fruits; tomatoes (tinned or pureed); one or two tins of baby food (pureed fruits) to add variety to dessert recipes.

COOKERY BOOKS

Many women will admit that they still go on cooking the same type of meals, and almost the same quantity, as when they had a whole family to feed. Cooking for only one or two is now better catered for by cookery books. Michelle Berriedale-Johnson, whose interesting recipes are featured on London Broadcasting Corporation radio, has produced a booklet called *Simply Simple Recipes*. These include a fruit cake that can be made in a saucepan, a chicken hotpot which also provides soup for the next day and a rice pudding cooked in a thermos flask. She favours casserole cooking with everything in one pot, as a change from the meat-and-two-veg. routine and emphasises the difference a little wine or sherry can make to a very simple dish.

Check-out books at supermarkets can be a useful source for ideas for inexpensive meals, and other handy guides are *Looking After Yourself in Retirement* and *Food for Thought* issued by the Health Education Council.

A hot drink in a hurry? Boiling water, beef essence and a tablespoon of dry sherry make a quick pick-me-up in icy weather. So does a glass of hot toddy: 3 teaspoonsful of honey, a slice of lemon, a pinch of cinnamon, a measure of rum or whisky, topped up with boiling water and well stirred.

VITAMINS

Do you need supplements? Views differ on this, as some hold that a balanced diet will contain everything you need, while others apply the belt-and-braces approach, taking extra vitamins and other supplements to make sure that the balance is maintained. Most older people find a multi-vitamin once daily, with or without iron, and cod-liver oil tablets in autumn and winter, are beneficial.

SMOKING AND DRINKING

If you have been in the habit, when working, of having a drink at lunch time, you will miss the convivial company as much as the beer or short drink. Fix up with a friend who has also retired to meet for a pre-lunch drink or an early evening one. A well-cooked meal waiting at home will be an incentive to make it a reasonably quick one and not spin it out till closing time.

Alcohol in reasonable quantity has a useful part to play. A sherry before a meal, a stout with a ploughman's lunch, or a small brandy-and-water at bedtime all have a role in aiding digestion and helping older people to relax.

By the time you are 50-plus you will have made your own decision about smoking. There is no doubt that heavy smokers are more at risk from bronchitis and circulatory troubles. Apart from the temporary withdrawal symptoms, no one ever suffered from giving up smoking. Those who decide to do so react in very different ways. Some can pack it up as soon as they make the decision, but others find it easier to cut down gradually, rationing themselves to fewer and fewer cigarettes.

If it is not an emergency, for example if you are acting under strict orders from the doctor, a useful incentive to give up is to choose something specific to save for, such as a greenhouse for the garden or an extra-special holiday. If you keep a close tab on the cash you have saved, even after a week or two you will be surprised at the total.

Everyone has a favourite recipe for cutting out smoking. The most efficient we have come across was a smoker who decided to suck a mint every time he wanted a cigarette. After a time he began to crave for the mints as much as he had previously done for a smoke. Then, one day he bought some own-brand mints from a well-known chain store. These were so horrible that he was cured, at one go, of the mint habit.

3 MONEY MATTERS

Money is important. Provided adequate provision has been made for a pension, and some savings have been set aside, you should have enough to enjoy life to the full now that you have more leisure time and opportunity to develop interests outside work.

The maximum pension which can be obtained is two-thirds of your final renumeration. Of course, this does not mean that you will only have spendable income of two-thirds of your former salary; the difference in *after tax* terms may be considerably less. Furthermore, you will also be entitled to the State Pension.

You should also bear in mind that you will no longer have certain types of expenses. An obvious example is that you will no longer need to pay out for a season ticket or for petrol in order to get to work. Also, many people move into a smaller house after retirement, so expenditure on rates, repairs, light and heat may be somewhat less.

It will take some time for your position to become clear after you retire. Initially there may be certain 'one-off' expenses, such as a long-promised holiday abroad. What you should do is to sit down before you retire and budget for your *expected* expenditure. When you arrive at a figure, you should add 15 per cent to allow a margin for expenditure that you may underestimate (it is rather surprising how smaller additional items can add up). After you have been retired for, say, a year you should sit down and repeat the exercise in the light of your *actual* expenditure. You will probably be surprised to find that you have surplus income but it is better to find yourself pleasantly surprised in this way rather than approach the financial adjustments of retirement in a random way.

If you have approached retirement shrewdly, you will have invested your savings for capital appreciation (after all, in the past, additional *taxable* income may have been an embarrassment to you). Now that the big day has arrived, you can start to reorganise your capital so as to produce progressively more income. However, don't lose sight of the need to preserve the value of your capital. You do need more income, but people have a longer life expectancy these days and even a relatively low rate of inflation can produce problems in 10 years time. Of every 1,000 single males who attain the age of 60, over 300 can expect to reach 80. With a married couple, the life expectancy for both parties is even greater – and you only have to think of what inflation has done over the last 20 years to see the need to keep some of your capital invested for capital growth.

Making full use of your capital (including any capital that you have raised by commuting part of your pension) really comes down to striking the right balance. A person aged 50 who is planning ahead should be aiming almost completely at getting capital appreciation; a person aged 60 who is about to retire should be moving into gilts and other income-producing assets, say 50 per cent invested for capital appreciation. And when you get to 70, the emphasis on getting income should be even more marked.

GOING BACK TO BASICS

The above has set the scene. Retirement need not bring financial worries as long as you have made proper provision. However, your aim once you retire should not simply be to maximise your income in the short term but rather to get some protection against the great enemy, inflation. We now need to go back and look at the various ingredients of your post-retirement income.

State Pensions

A state pension will not in itself be enough for you to live comfortably in retirement. However, for most people it is the one inflation-proofed investment that they have.

A person retiring at the present time will have a pension made up of two parts:

1. *The basic flat rate retirement pension.* In the UK this is currently (November 1985) £1,991.60 per annum for a single person or £3,187.60 for a married couple where the wife has not made sufficient contributions. If your wife has worked and has sufficient National Insurance contributions,

she can receive the full single person's pension in her own right, i.e. you can each receive £1,991.60. The basic-rate pension is raised by the Government in line with the retail price index in November of each year.

2. *The earnings-related scheme.* You should also be entitled to additional benefits from the State earnings-related scheme (unless you are contracted out of this scheme because your company pension gives you equivalent benefits).

Benefits under this scheme are related to your salary. A person is entitled to a pension at the rate of 1.25 per cent of his earnings between the lower and upper limits for each year of contributions since April 1978. In 1984/85, the lower earnings limit was £147.33 per month and the upper limit was £183.33. Each year's earnings are revalued annually until retirement, in line with movements in national average earnings. This means that a person retiring now who has contributed at the maximum rate since 1978 will be entitled to receive an annual pension of something like £1,000 per annum. After retirement, the pension is index-linked.

In relation to the earnings-related scheme, in the June 1985 Green Paper it was proposed that the State earnings-related pension scheme (SERPS) should be replaced by a compulsory occupational pension scheme. The White Paper published in December 1985 abandoned this concept in favour of moral and financial persuasions to employers to set up schemes to top up a reduced SERPS. Under the original SERPS, replacement of State benefits by occupational scheme benefits by contracting-out was permitted only if the occupational scheme satisfied an extensive set of tests, designed to ensure that the employee could never be worse off as a result of contracting-out.

Under the new agreement the State is to allow contracting-out on less stringent terms. Thus more of the responsibility for the adequacy of an employee's retirement provision was passed to employers and the employees themselves.

The changes discussed are being phased in over a long period. Nobody reaching State pension age this century should be affected by the changes to SERPS. On the assumptions of the December White Paper it is being taken that earnings will rise faster than prices and, on the forecast basis, the fall in State provision will be accounted for more by the reduction in the value of the basic pension relative to earnings than by the reduction in SERPS benefits in years to come. This is because the basic pension is increased only in line with prices. Other changes to SERPS will reduce the pension of those who have experienced substantial real changes in their earnings over their careers, in particular those with long periods of unemployment.

The Social Security Bill was published in January 1986, following the

December 1985 White Paper. It is likely to be extensively amended as it goes through Parliament, and it is impossible to forecast its final form. It is worth noting that the right to make additional voluntary contributions when belonging to an occupational pension scheme, is likely to be made an entitlement.

Company Pensions
In order for a person to be contracted out of the State earnings-related scheme, he must be a member of a company pension scheme which provides equivalent or better benefits.

Apart from this, the legislation is concerned to ensure that you don't derive excessive benefits and does not impose minimum levels. The Inland Revenue permit pension schemes to be approved which provide a pension at normal retirement date of two-thirds of the person's final salary (subject to a minimum of 10 years' service). In practice, most schemes provide a pension related to the length of service on the basis of 1/60th of final salary for each year of service. Thus, in most cases, you will earn the maximum pension only if you have been working for the company for 40 years.

From a practical point of view, as you approach the last year of your employment, you should contact your employer, study any literature given to you in connection with the company's pension scheme and establish your prospective benefits.

What Can Be Done To Enhance Benefits?
Many pension schemes enable employees who will not earn the maximum pension (because the scheme provides for benefits based on the 1/60th principle) to purchase additional pension benefits by making additional voluntary contributions. These are contributions which attract tax relief and are the best type of guaranteed investment that you could possibly have. The maximum sum which may be contributed in this way is a figure which, together with any other contributions that you may make under the scheme, totals 15 per cent of your salary for the year.

This book is concerned with coping with retirement, or making the most of it. To succeed in this, preparation for retirement is the first step. Those interested should look into such matters and transfer values, additional voluntary contributions and so on while still in their 50s.

Self-Employed?
A self-employed person can obtain tax relief for contributions into an

34

approved retirement annuity contract. If you fall into this category you should seriously consider setting aside the maximum 17½ per cent contributions permitted for people born in or after 1934. The maximum percentage of earnings for people born between 1916 and 1933 is 20 per cent and, for anyone still working and born before 1916, the rates are slightly higher still; in fact, the higher maximum percentages range from 21 per cent for people born in 1915 to 32½ per cent for people born in 1907. If you have not made the maximum payments in earlier years you can catch up now as tax relief is available for payments which match the unused relief for the last 6 years. However, hurry up: the sooner you invest in a gross fund which is exempt, the more you will accumulate for retirement.

Commuting Part Of Your Pension

It is normal for a person at retirement to be given the option of taking a tax-free lump sum instead of part of his pension entitlement. This is a very valuable benefit but many people are not sure whether it is really best to cash in their pension and take this lump sum.

In our experience, it is normally beneficial, *unless* the company pension is likely to be regularly reviewed to take account of inflation. If a lump sum is taken and invested in gilts, the effect on your immediate income is likely to be negligible and you will always have access to this capital. Also, for a married man, it is a way of providing the maximum income for his wife if he pre-deceases her. And gilts are only one way of investing the capital. If your residual pension is sufficient for your present needs it may well make sense to invest part of the capital sum for growth.

INVESTING YOUR CAPITAL
Taxation

You must not let tax considerations dictate to you. Investment considerations and long-term returns are much more important than saving tax in the short term. However, you should be aware of the trap that arises because of the rules for age allowance.

Age allowance is an additional allowance available to those aged 65 or more during the tax year. The allowance in 1985/86 is £2,690 for a single person and £4,255 for a married person. This allowance is reduced where the person or couple's total income exceeds £8,800, with the allowance being reduced by £2 for every £3 of income above this sum. When the total income for married couples reaches £10,000 per year, the effect of the £2 for £3 reduction is that the age allowance is reduced to the normal personal allowance, and thus the benefit of age allowance is lost. The effect of this is that you may pay tax at 50 per cent on the income which takes you over the £8,800 limit. (For single persons the benefit eases at £9,527.)

Capital Gains v. Income

You should also bear in mind that capital gains are taxed more lightly than income. The maximum rate, and the only rate for individuals is 30 per cent which is the same as the basic rate of income tax, but the first £5,900 capital gains are exempt each year.

Types Of Investments Available

What follows is descriptive rather than prescriptive in that, at the last analysis, it is you who must determine the right balance between income and capital-growth investments.

Banks And Building Societies

These are obviously the most popular types of investment. Their emotional attraction is that they are as 'safe as houses'. On the other hand, whilst your capital is secure, you could almost certainly do better from an income point of view *in the long term*. The point is that interest rates may well fall away in the next few years and it makes sense therefore to safeguard your income position for the next 5 years – at least with part of your capital. This is certainly what has happened in the past as Table 1 demonstrates.

Table 1   Return from £10,000 invested in a Building Society

	Annual Interest	Retail Price Index
1975	£ 871	100
1980	£1200	364
1984	£ 853	475

Building Societies do permit you to take some safeguards but only to a limited extent. A number of Building Societies provide 2- or 3-year bonds which pay interest at a rate which is guaranteed to be 2 per cent or 3 per cent better than the ordinary-share rate. However, this is unlikely to be the complete answer; after all, what do you do in 3 years' time?

Nevertheless, any financial advisor will recognise that there is a place for Building-Society investments for the older investor. They are a very good home for money which you may need for expenditure in the short term, money which you would like to keep available for investment opportunities which arise from time to time, and many older people also feel that they need an emergency fund available to meet any unforeseen expenditure. But do not be too cautious. £10,000 is probably quite sufficient for all these purposes and, if you keep more than that in the Building Society, you are not really making your money work as hard for you as it could. Remember that you had to work hard to accumulate your money in the first place, so you want it to work as hard as possible for you now, provided of course that this does not involve undue risk.

Government Stock

Government stock, or 'gilts' (so called because of the appearance of the stock certificate) can provide certain guarantees for long-term income. The rate of return is fixed by interest rates at the time when you invest, and you can be assured that you will have this income for the time that you hold the stocks. If you buy stock which will not be redeemed for 5 or 10 years you are *guaranteed* that level of income until redemption.

Of course, gilts are not the complete answer any more than anything else. It is true that you secure a given level of return for the life of the stock, but if you need access to your capital in the meantime you may incur a loss. Equally, you might make a profit. The point is that the value of Government stock between the date of issue and its redemption date is liable to fluctuation. However, the fluctuation as not so great as is the case with shares. Also, as Government stocks approach 5 years of their redemption date, the price obtainable in the market gets closer and closer to the redemption value. So an investment of £15–20,000 out of capital of £50,000 may well make sense.

Gilts pay interest half-yearly so it can be appropriate to purchase several different stocks so as to have an even flow of income throughout the year.

Another aspect is the life of the stock. Many investors like to invest in Government stocks of different duration, i.e. one with 5 years to redemption, one with 7 years and one with a 10-year life. In this way, they can be assured that capital will be released at regular intervals, thus smoothing out cash flow.

Very often Government stocks can be purchased at a discount so that their redemption value produces a profit. These profits are normally completely tax-free and can be used to supplement income or to help preserve the real value of your capital.

National Savings Certificates

National Savings Certificates can be a good alternative to gilts. They afford a guaranteed tax-free return over a 5-year period. Equally, there are index-linked national savings certificates which could be worth considering as a hedge against inflation. Clearly you will not want to tie up most of your capital in this way, but a modest investment (say £5,000 out of a portfolio of £50,000) could make a lot of sense. The maximum that you can invest is £5,000 *in each issue* (there have been thirty-three separate issues) so you could invest quite considerable sums over a period, but £5,000 *in total* is probably enough unless you are very wealthy.

Equities

Ordinary shares, or 'equities' as they are generally called, have proved a marvellous hedge against inflation over the last 10 years. Whether they are an attractive proposition given the present historically-high level of the Stock Market is another matter, but this really comes down to the question of *timing*. There is certainly a case for putting some of your capital in equities, but it is obviously a matter of judgment as to whether you invest now or wait to see whether the market will be lower in 6 months' time. You should consult a stockbroker, bank manager or other advisor on this.

For a person with capital of £50,000, individual investments in stocks and shares are unlikely to be the most effective way of going about things. Unit trusts offer an attractive alternative whereby you can invest

Table 2   Typical Return from an Investment in 1975
(Income net of basic rate tax, on £13,870 invested 1/1/75)

	Shares	Building Societies
1975	£1130	£1000
1976	£1220	£ 960
1977	£1420	£ 970
1978	£1680	£ 870
1979	£1970	£1170
1980	£2210	£1450
1981	£2200	£1260
1982	£2450	£1180
1983	£2620	£ 940
1984	£3010	£ 970
	Capital Values after 10 years	
	+293%	+0%
	Which is the risky investment?	

(*Figures extrapolated from the* de Zoete Equity-Gilt Study *by Martin Tryczynki of Allied Dunbar*)

in equities and yet have a 'spread' so that you are not dependent on the fortunes of just one or two companies. If you have invested most of your £50,000 with building societies, gilts, national savings certificates, etc, you should think seriously of investing around £15,000 in unit trusts as these offer the chance for capital growth. Table 2 speaks for itself.

Insurance Bonds

These are similar in investment terms to unit trusts although the tax treatment is fundamentally different. The insurance element is minimal; basically an investor acquires units and the death benefit corresponds to the value of those units. The investment can be cashed in and the surrender value is normally 100 per cent of the value of the units.

Insurance bonds offer a broader range of investments than unit trusts in that it is possible to invest in property funds and other specialised funds.

Furthermore, insurance companies provide a managed fund which is a fund where the managers themselves have the discretion on the way in which the fund is invested between property, gilts, equities and so on. In practice, most people opt for the managed fund and it is fair to say that these funds have produced steady growth over the past few years. It must be said that they have on average produced less growth than unit trusts, but then they are more broadly based and, when the Stock Market has taken a down turn, the managed funds have not been hit so heavily.

Some aspects of the tax treatment of insurance bonds are favourable. For example unless you are subject to higher rates there is no tax to pay whatsoever on amounts that you withdraw from insurance bonds nor is the overall profit when you cash in the bond entirely taxable. But be careful that the profit on an insurance bond does not take you into the higher-rate bands as tax could then be payable.

It is also fair to point out that insurance bonds are less favourably treated 'internally' than unit trusts. Unit trusts are funds which are free from capital-gains tax so the managers can switch around without any tax inhibitions. Insurance-bond funds are subject to a capital-gains tax charge and the fund's liability for this has to be passed on to the investor in the way in which the unit price is calculated. For the modest investor with capital of £50,000 it is unlikely that a personal liability for capital-gains tax will arise and therefore unit trusts offer a more tax-efficient way of investment.

To some extent the tax treatment is secondary. What matters is that money that you have invested in risk investments such as unit trusts, equities, property funds and so on are professionally managed. Properly monitored they should produce capital growth over a reasonable period, but the emphasis is on 'properly monitored'. It is not sufficient to invest in a unit trust and then forget about it, apart from collecting your 6-monthly dividend cheque. Investments need to be managed and you need to review the position regularly with a specialist such as a stockbroker. Some people find this a strain and would rather delegate investment management to an insurance company and, for these people, insurance bonds can be an appropriate investment.

We have concentrated very much in this chapter on someone who will have capital available for investment of around £50,000. If you have less than half that assumed capital the same general principles will apply, the actual sums being scaled down proportionately. One must take a very conservative approach in both these cases and look primarily to types of investment that will produce a guaranteed return.

Of course, for people who have more capital a different strategy is appropriate. If you have capital of £100,000, it may well make sense to have half of it invested in unit trusts and, for people with more capital than that, it can be appropriate to have investments in specific stocks and shares. Many firms of stockbrokers are more than happy to offer a personal service to clients of this nature and to manage a portfolio designed for your particular requirements.

Charges
Building Societies make no charges for an investment. Nor does the Department of National Savings. But as we have seen, the investments offered by Building Societies and the Department of National Savings cannot satisfy your full requirements. They are all right as part of an investment plan, but you do need to have some money invested for capital growth.

A stockbroker or bank may charge for purchasing gilts but the charge is modest; as an indication an investment of £10,000 in a Government stock means paying the stockbroker a charge of £37 (plus VAT). The charges for buying and selling shares are higher, more like £165. It is, of course, possible to buy many gilts through the Post Office, and this is the cheapest method of all.

If you invest in unit trusts or insurance bonds you are unlikely to have to pay a fee. There is a 'hidden charge' in that the price at which you buy units is usually 5 per cent or 6 per cent more than the price at which you sell them back to the company. Part of the reason for that change is to enable a fee to be paid to an advisor such as a stockbroker, insurance broker etc. Many people find it slightly disturbing that an advisor may receive 3–5 per cent of the sum invested, but you must remember that nothing of value in this world really comes for free and there is a price to pay for good advice. Provided that the investment has been carefully chosen, the 'front end' charge will come down to a fairly low percentage looked at over the period of the investment. However, there is no need to feel awkward about asking for more advice; you should calculate what the advisor stands to make out of your business and then take care to ensure that you receive an appropriate amount of benefit in terms of time spent discussing your affairs, analysing your requirements and picking an appropriate investment.

Home-Income Plans – Turning your House Into An Annuity

Many people invest most of their capital in their homes, thinking that when they retire the property can be sold and the proceeds used to supplement their income, However, in practice, many people eventually decide to stay put and consequently this source of income-producing capital is not available to them. One option which should be considered in this situation is for the people to use their home to provide income through a Home-Income scheme.

Essentially, these schemes work as follows:

1. The home-owner takes a mortgage on the property of up to £30,000 on an interest-only basis. Tax relief is available provided at least 90 per cent of the amount raised is used to buy an annuity.
2. The person purchases an annuity which is sufficient to cover the interest on the mortgage and to leave enough to provide additional spendable income.
3. When the person dies the house is sold and the mortgage is repaid. The sale proceeds, less the outstanding mortgage, pass to the person's beneficiaries.

Whilst these schemes have their attractions, it must be recognised that they are really only suitable for the elderly. A single person normally has to be at least 70 years of age and a married couple must have a combined age of 150 before these schemes are viable.

As an example of the level of income that can be produced, a 70-year-old woman arranging a £25,000 loan would receive annual spendable income of £935 if she pays tax at the basic rate. Provided that you are in the right age bracket, and have a property worth more than £15,000, you could consider such a scheme. You may feel misgivings about the possible loss of capital to your family if you were to die in the short term, but this can be overcome. A £25,000 plan on a 'capital-protected' basis would still yield spendable income of £870.

NOTE: The advice given in this chapter assumes an investment of around £50,000. If only £25,000 is available, then the advice would be to be more cautious and pay more attention to obtaining a guaranteed income. If even less is available, then it is even more important to avoid risks and try to obtain the maximum guaranteed return. Conversely, the more money available above £50,000, the more accent can be placed on seeking capital growth with the prospect of a higher income in the future.

4 MOVING

Houses, like clothes, can be outgrown. The roomy home, once full of teenagers and their friends can suddenly become an empty barracks, largely unused but still hungry for heat and in constant need of maintenance. Yet many people, on retirement, cling to it as something familiar in a world where they have already had to face one major change – that of ending their working life.

It is not surprising that half the people who retire continue to live in the same building in which they brought up a family. What is surprising is that more people do not put it to better use. An accountant once told us: 'For most people their home is the greatest asset they're ever likely to own. I can't understand why so many get the absolute minimum of value out of it'.

Often people confuse moving home with moving away from a locality. The idea of trekking out to other areas, armed with sheaves of misleading information from estate agents, is sufficient to make them say: 'We're probably as well off here as anywhere'. They foresee a major upheaval, leaving friends in one town and having to start a new circle of acquaintances in another. There is also the problem of finding a new doctor, dentist or bank manager as helpful as those they already know.

STAYING PUT
Having looked at the situation and decided that 'here' is as good as anywhere, it is time to take note of the very wide range of options open to those who choose to stay put.

Converting Your House Into Flats

A large mature house can be converted into flats, sometimes with the help of a local government grant, keeping one apartment for yourself and letting the rest. This can be fairly costly, but you have the future rents to offset against the initial capital expenditure. It can also be quite an upheaval, so it is sometimes necessary to move out temporarily while the major work is being carried out in order to avoid the noise and dust. Some friends of ours hired a caravan which was temporarily installed in their long garden. This allowed them to live comfortably on site, keeping an eye on the progress of the work.

Generally it takes at least 2 or 3 months for planning permission to go through for such a conversion, so to get a clear run of fine summer weather it is necessary to seek planning permission around February/March or even earlier. For any sizable property it pays to employ an architect or surveyor, to get the permission and to see the job through with the builder and sub-contractors.

If you decide on this course, it is a good idea to have all the major work done before retirement, while earnings are still coming in.

At present – 1985 – government grants are largely restricted to essential repairs to homes built before 1919, but even this can show a considerable saving when it comes to roofing and guttering, damp-proofing and drains. Council requirements vary considerably. One couple we know, living in the Greater London Council area, wanted to convert a small Edwardian house into two self-contained flats. However, when they discovered the list of requirements, they thought better of it and settled for summer holiday lettings which provide an income to meet rates, exterior painting and whole-house background heating in the colder months. Had they continued with a full conversion, they would have had to provide fire-retardant materials for doors and partitioning of the stairs, hardboarding of all the upper floor, and would have had to meet a large bill from the water authority for bringing water across the road to provide an entirely separate supply for the upstairs flat. But the thing which decided them against conversion was the fact that all the local estate agents advised that they would be devaluing their property, as in that particular area there was a glut of small flats and a shortage of compact four-bedroom houses.

Sharing Your House

An alternative to conversion is to share the house with other members of your family or with friends, or to take in one or more lodgers. All these options need to be approached with caution. Even the most closely-knit families can grate on each other if clear demarcation lines are not drawn right at the beginning. The areas likely to give rise to most irritation are kitchens and bathrooms. It is much less expensive to turn a small bedroom into a kitchen, or to install a second bathroom or a shower room on the ground floor, than to face a major conversion. Yet the effects can be enormously important.

Next in the priority order is sound-insulation. Some people like to live in a household with plenty of hubbub. They do not worry about upstairs, noisy radio because their own is on at full blast. But for the majority, although it is reassuring to hear signs of life around the place, it is more restful if they are just a faint background murmur.

If there is a rear as well as a front entrance, arrange it so that one household has most of its comings and goings from the back of the house while the other uses the front for exits and entrances. This avoids the irritation of younger people, rushing off to work or coming back laden from the shops, at being waylaid by older ones whose feelings can be hurt by the brusque ending of what they had hoped would be a leisurely chat.

Exchanging Your House
There are other ways of remaining in the same locality and not severing all local links. You can exchange a larger house or flat for something smaller, either privately owned or through the local council. It will usually take quite a few months, but as a number of people like to plan their retirement well before they actually pack up work, they can put a deal of this type through and avoid the hassle of a chain of buyers and sellers. In this way, you have the bonus of a new home, which is easier and cheaper to run, while still being in touch with friends.

Letting Your House And Renting
Another possibility which should not be overlooked is letting your house furnished and renting a smaller home on a similar basis for yourself. This definitely would not suit everyone, but is a way of retaining your valuable asset and making a profit on it. This option tends to favour those who travel light, who would be content to leave larger items – furniture and appliances – to their tenants, and set off with books, favourite ornaments, and other personal paraphernalia into a new and more compact home. We know people who have done this for a 'let' of 3 years or so, and then been happy to return to the old home, refreshed by the change. There are others who find the arrangement so convenient

45

that they have continued with the tenancy over a very long time, reaping a modest profit from the difference in rent between their large house and the smaller one they are now renting.

Whatever you do, it is essential to employ a solicitor and a reliable agent and to have a well-drawn-up tenancy agreement. Advertisements on cards in newsagents may sometimes be all right when looking for a lodger, but something more watertight is necessary before strangers can be allowed to take over the whole of your house. Most tenancy agreements follow the same lines, with a stated length of notice at the end. Never make the mistake of sharing the same solicitor. This is sometimes done to save two lots of fees, but no lawyer can fully represent the interests of both parties. One of his duties will be to make you fully aware of the implications of the latest Acts governing furnished and unfurnished lettings. On the whole, these still tend to favour the tenant, but not to the same extent which they did some years ago. The role of the letting agent varies according to a sliding scale of commission. In return, he undertakes to find suitable tenants, to take up references, to ensure regular payment of the rent and to visit the premises at stated intervals to inspect their condition. The more service he provides, the higher the fee. Before you leave the house it will be necessary to make an inventory covering all the items which have to be accounted for at the end of the tenancy. Inevitably there will be some deterioration in the premises and their contents, even with the best tenants, so account should be taken of this in fixing a realistic rent.

The most popular form of letting with many people is the company let. In this case the tenancy agreement is made with a firm and the landlord deals with the company's letting officer rather than with a series of tenants. If you are interested in this approach, it is essential to investigate the prospects of company lets in your area. Some firms are only interested in larger properties or in apartments in blocks of flats where there are very good security arrangements and the services of a caretaker or porter.

Buying A Smaller Property
One of the most simple options – and one which a large number of people would choose – is that of selling the house and buying a smaller house, still in the same area. The difference between the selling price and the buying price can show a profit which can be invested, although proper allowance must be made for moving expenses. These would, of course, be lower if you were only a few streets away. Although the onus is on the house-buyer to find out what is and what is not included in the

sale, the estate agent should inform him what is to be removed by the seller. So, if selling, you should make it clear to the agent what is to be kept and what is to be included in the sale or sold separately. If buying, check this inventory carefully before exchanging contracts.

Another option is to buy a flat. This might not appeal to keen gardeners, but is a practical solution for a couple who have both been out at work and whose present home has been mainly used at evenings and weekends. A flat in a block provides company for retired business people, especially when there are communal services such as a restaurant and bar, swimming pool or games room.

Even the keenest gardener may be forced by health reasons to give up a large garden. A widower we know, troubled for some time with arthritis, was determined to avoid the misery of seeing his big garden deteriorate because he could no longer keep up the high standards he set himself. His first move was to a bungalow with an ample but smaller garden and for some years he enjoyed looking after this. As he became older and less able to put in all the work needed, he decided to move again, and this time the garden is a small one attached to a ground-floor maisonette. It is well within his capacity to maintain and, in return for digging and manuring by younger neighbours, he supplies them with cuttings and seedlings, as well as with strawberries from his small greenhouse.

If considering a bungalow as the first option on retirement, one of the major advantages is the lack of stairs. This is particularly important if the illness of one partner involves the other in carrying trays up and down stairs at frequent intervals. The second advantage is that even roof maintenance can be carried out by a fit do-it-yourselfer in his 60s. There is no need to worry about costly repainting of woodwork, or about choked gutters or loose tiles, when they can be reached by a single-section ladder or even a tall pair of steps. Another point is that all the windows can be kept sparkling clean. In many areas it is rare to find a window-cleaner and there is nothing more dispiriting than looking out of blurred and dingy windows when you wake in the morning. In a bungalow, with all rooms on the ground floor, it is possible to see to this job yourself.

For people who have friends or family coming on regular visits, a chalet bungalow is worth considering. This provides guest accommodation whenever needed, while the ground floor continues to function undisturbed. It can also provide useful storage space for extra bedding, winter clothes in summer and vice versa, helping to keep other rooms tidy and easy to clean. Gardening has already been mentioned and bungalows offer a varying range of garden sizes, from extensive lawns and flower beds to something not much bigger than a patio.

When buying and selling it is as well to remember that, generally, in a garden the trees, shrubs and plants are regarded as part of the sale. Garden sheds and greenhouses built on foundations are usually fixtures, but freestanding ones can be taken away by the seller. The position is uncertain regarding very heavy garden ornaments or stone seats. Sometimes they are taken to be fixtures because of their weight, but at other times are considered to be movable because they are freestanding. Fitted kitchens with built-in ovens and split-level hobs are probably taken to be fixtures, but the same does not apply to freestanding fridges, dishwashers and washing machines. These can, of course, be sold separately apart from the house sale. That also applies to any electrical apparatus using a detachable plug, e.g. electric fires. But gas fires might be considered fixtures if removing them entails making good. Light fittings have often raised problems, but generally the sockets, wall switches and wiring come within the sale, but not lampshades and bulbs. Carpets and curtains are often included in the sale nowadays, or can be offered separately. Unless very expensive indeed, it is often better economics to leave them and buy fresh for your new home or accept those you will find there until you can replace them later.

You should always keep a record of your property and the appliances within it, together with all manuals for appliances, addresses of builders who have carried out work, and a note of floor and window sizes. This will be useful when getting further work done or if something goes wrong. It is also handy for the person buying the place, who needs the fullest possible information, especially if he is a DIY enthusiast. A very efficient log-book for homes is published by Davenport, Kingdom & Co. and provides for everything you need to record, including heating, fuel, insulation, drainage, mains services and so on.

If you still find the idea of house-hunting intimidating, there are 'legwork' agencies which will make work easier. If supplied with a detailed specification of your requirements, they will shortlist properties within that category, saving you wasted time and petrol or train fares. Several of these relocation agencies can be found among regular advertisers in the weekly magazine *Country Life*.

For someone who would like to change from a roast beef/two veg. semi in the suburbs to a period house, the best way to find out what is available is through the *Period Property Register*. Not all period homes are in the millionaire bracket, but some need a lot of money to be spent on them.

48

Building Your Own Home

If you have looked forward for years to building a dream home, now is the chance to do it. But be prepared for snags. One golden rule is that everything costs more than the estimate and everything takes twice as long as promised. Murphy's Law operates in this field just as it does everywhere else. If the new home is to be built in your existing locality, at least there is a better chance of keeping an eye on the work and avoiding the expense of long-distance telephone calls and visits to find out what is happening. You also have the opportunity of seeing other examples of the architect's work, and of knowing something about the contractors he employs.

Home-Income Plan

An alternative to staying put and letting property deteriorate because you cannot afford to pay for maintenance or do it yourself is the 'home-income' plan discussed in Chapter 3 whereby you raise a capital sum to finance essential repairs and get a monthly income to supplement your pension. At present this is only available to those aged 70 or over, if single, or to couples whose combined age is over 150. Basically, the building society lends up to 65 per cent of the value of the property, the sum being used to buy an annuity, with up to 10 per cent of the amount to be paid at once, in a lump sum, for repairs, while the annuity pays out a set amount each month.

TAKING UP ROOTS

A large number of people, though not so great as the stay-putters, decide to move away from their own neighbourhood. This is especially so when living there was largely dictated by a job or by the children's schools.

Moving Closer To Relatives

One of the most familiar moves for a retired couple is to sell up and go to live very close to a married son or daughter. It *can* work, and frequently does, but it is just as likely to lead to problems, and a home not quite so near to the young marrieds could be a better choice. It is difficult for parents to realise that their children are grown up, and it is equally difficult for young marrieds not to take too much advantage of a free baby-sitting service always on tap. It is true that grandparents welcome the company of their grandchildren, but they do not need it all the time. Another point is that, in the 20–40 years age band, promotion very often involves a move to another area, and it would be extremely disappointing to uproot yourself and find a few months later that your son or daughter had had to go to the other end of the country, or even further afield.

If you are going to move to be near other members of the family, it makes more sense to be in closer touch with a brother or sister. A lot of distress is caused to people in their 60s who hear of their contemporaries struggling on during ill health and having to depend on the kindness of neighbours. There is frequently a feeling of guilt that the family has not rallied round, whereas in fact very often they are not in a position to do so. But they could be available to help, if only the brother or sister lived close by. In the days of large families this problem did not exist; there was always someone who could be dispatched to look after the ailing relative, and many families, although living in separate houses, tended to group themselves in a close-knit local community.

Moving To A Holiday Town

The next most familiar reason for a move is to return to a place where you have spent very enjoyable holidays over the years. This sounds attractive and can be so, but make sure of it by going to stay in the area at the worst time of year. November or February are likely to be the grimmer months. If it is a seaside town, do not stay in a comfortable hotel, but take inexpensive lodgings or an economical self-catering flat. Then spend a good deal of time walking around the area. You may find that the rainswept front with its peeling posters of long-gone shows, and the doleful groups of people attending conferences at out-of-season rates, will make you take a new look at things. It was probably in November or February that King George V uttered his famous remark 'Bugger Bognor'.

Dream Cottages

The dream of a country cottage off the beaten track is very much a thing of the past. Ninety-nine per cent of these were bought up in the 1950s by smart developers. If you come across a derelict property and still want to turn it into something delightful, then go very carefully indeed into all the possible snags. If you find one completely modernised, with town gas electricity and mains drainage, it will cost as much as one of the same size in a more convenient location, where it would not be essential to run a car and where the doctor could come quickly in case of emergency.

The south-east coastline of England harbours more people of retirement age than in any other part of the country. This has its advantages. More attention is paid to the needs and tastes of those over 60 and even to those who are really elderly. In Surrey, Hampshire and

Dorset, the weather is generally good, although in the case of Kent it can be very severe at times. But there is the snag that prices tend to be higher, with fewer wage-earners and industrial concerns to provide a cushion for the rates. As older people tend to consult their doctors more often, it also means that medical facilities can be overloaded.

Sheltered Housing

Another choice could be sheltered housing, with your own home and furniture, privacy and independence, but a warden on call in case any problems arise. There are a few freehold schemes but the majority are for leases from 60 to 999 years. The New Homes Board can supply a list of developers building sheltered homes with warden service. The variety of sheltered housing is considerable. It may be an estate of newly-built houses, maisonettes or bungalows. A large mansion may be split into apartments and the outbuildings, such as stables, barns and gardeners' cottages, also converted. The cost of the properties is on a par with that of a small house, with buyers meeting the normal outgoings of rates and heating and lighting, as well as an annual contribution to the upkeep of the gardens and the services of a warden. Should you wish to sell and move away at any time, you can do so, and the house or flat can be bequeathed in the normal way.

A typical scheme may comprise some ten or twenty one-bedroom or two-bedroom flats or bungalows of similar size. Locations are chosen for access to shops, banks, post offices, churches and public transport.

In other schemes of sheltered housing, flats and bungalows are leased for the life of the tenant, or jointly in the case of a married couple. On the death of the remaining tenant the purchase price, without deductions, goes to the heirs. If the property has risen in value, they do not benefit from this, but against that the retired couple have been spared the cost of repairs, maintenance and insurance, and have had the benefit of a resident warden's services.

Services available to residents vary a great deal. One housing association includes building insurance, window-cleaning, gardening and the use of washing machines and tumble dryers among the facilities. The warden deals with health visitors and the DHSS regarding pensions and checks to see that everyone is in good health. If anyone is away on holiday, she will water indoor plants or feed the fish. Some sheltered schemes provide a guest room which can be booked for overnight visitors and also include a residents' lounge. If looking round a scheme, check on the following points: worktops, shelves, cupboards, electric sockets and light switches at a convenient height; hand-rails on stairs; grab-rails at the side of the bath; for flats of over two storeys a lift with space for a wheelchair.

Before making a decision, check that there is no risk of losing your sheltered home if your health deteriorates. The House Builders Federation advises: 'Leases should clearly state the level of care which will or will not be provided if the lessee or resident falls ill, is injured or becomes infirm either temporarily or permanently, when he/she is unable to continue to maintain an independent existence. Residents should be required to inform lessors of the names of their doctors and next of kin, and also to consent to appropriate assistance being called on their behalf by the management organisation should there be reasonable cause to suspect illness.' This sounds quite reasonable, as the warden is not there as a full-time nurse, but it is essential to know the exact terms of the contract if you or an elderly relative are planning to buy the lease of a sheltered home. It is also very important to know the range of social services available in the area, so that these can be provided by the local authority for those who have become more in need of support as time goes on.

Two useful publications on housing in retirement are Thames Television's *Staying Put or Moving On?* and *A Buyer's Guide to Sheltered Housing* by Age Concern and the National Housing and Town Planning Council. Older people may have pets from which they do not want to be separated. The latter guide advises: 'You normally have to obtain the written permission of the management organisation before you can bring in a pet.... If you have a pet you are strongly advised to ask the management organisation's attitude towards them before you buy'.

Sheltered housing is also provided by a number of councils, and there are at present some 200,000 of these homes, but waiting lists are extremely long so that application should be made as early as possible. Housing associations provide some 500,000 homes in the UK of which more than a third are for elderly people.

Private Hotels, Boarding Houses and Retirement Homes.
We have not mentioned two other options which come in a somewhat similar category. One is the private hotel or boarding house, which appeals to retired singles or couples who like the company of others of all ages rather than just their own generation. This can be the answer for those who no longer want the responsibility of running their own homes and, having sold them and invested the capital, can afford to live in modest comfort while others see to the chores. It is a solution for retired people in good health, as such places are not run with the needs of the

ailing elderly specifically in mind.

Retirement homes are geared to meet those needs and, again, they may be privately owned and therefore need to be run at a profit, financed by charitable trusts, or operated by local councils. Generally the accommodation consists of single bedrooms with their own wash-basins, and communal dining rooms and lounges. In some cases, residents are able to bring their own furniture. The homes vary enormously in price and quality, and are something which the newly retired can consider as a future possibility, or which they may need to investigate on behalf of their own elderly relatives – parents in their 80s who cannot be properly looked after by 60-year-old sons or daughters. Your own general practitioner is probably the best source of information on these places, and so is the district nurse, as their work takes them into the homes operating in your district. It is customary for prospective residents to be allowed to see over the homes initially, and quite usual for a short trial stay to be arranged. But, as we have said, this is something to be considered in the future. In the meantime, there is a further choice for the retired man or woman to make. That is whether to stay at home or to move abroad. This is dealt with in the next chapter.

5 MOVING ABROAD

Today a number of people in the UK already own a holiday apartment in a sunnier country and quite a few look forward to spending their retirement there.

Taking a quick survey of friends who have done this, we have found the score equally divided between those who have settled down happily and permanently, coming back to the UK for holidays from time to time, and those who have returned home disillusioned after only a few years.

Whether it is a matter of settling in the UK or abroad, the key word is 'realism'. Gone are the days of low-cost living, with plenty of cheap domestic service. By the time you have made the adjustments for respective levels of taxation – both direct and indirect – there is very little difference financially between staying put or living abroad. Locally-grown food may be absurdly cheap, but imported items can often be extremely dear, and this applies to everyday items and not just luxuries.

It is all right to stick to the region's beer and wines during a 2-week holiday, although your preference is for Scotch or for an ale not locally obtainable, but the attraction wears off if you have to do this for 365 days a year. As regards the cheap domestic help, it must not be forgotten that the tourist industry lures many thousands to work in the big hotels and holiday camps, so if you want a 'daily' you may have to look a long way and pay a much higher rate than in the past.

One thing you can generally be assured of is a steady stream of visitors from home. This provides plenty of company throughout the summer and allows you to hibernate in the winter when the weather is not so attractive. After all, it sometimes rains in the Canaries, and if you follow the sunshine tables in the daily newspapers and chart the maximum and minimum temperature levels and rainfall you will often find that Bournemouth or Worthing come much higher up than their equivalents in France, Italy or Spain. You can also write to the tourist office of the country concerned for the official government weather statistics.

Here are some of the points you should consider when weighing up the pros and cons of moving. Is the climate reliable – sunny and non-extreme? Is the area hilly or reasonably flat, making for easier walking for older people? What local transport is available? (you may not want to use a car all the time or may even decide to give up driving completely.) Is the cost of living favourable? Is the area top-heavy with elderly people or well balanced between various ages? All these apply equally in your own country. When moving abroad you can add the following: Are there reciprocal health service arrangements with the UK? Are you able to make yourself understood in the language? Is the regime politically stable and not basically hostile to British people? If you buy a house abroad, can you get your money out at a later date?

Everyone varies in their reaction to these questions. Some people actually look forward to the challenge of learning another language, adapting to a totally different environment, and welcoming a complete change from their former way of life. Others really seek the good points of the UK with the bonus of more sunshine and plenty of cheap vino. Should you decide to spend your retirement abroad, there are a number of essential steps to take.

FINANCIAL CONSIDERATIONS

The bank manager is the best person to advise on the amount of money which can be taken out of the UK. This has varied a certain amount and the rules have changed, over the years and also between the overseas sterling area and the rest of the globe. But in all cases, Bank of England permission is required, and information should be obtained either from them direct or via your bank manager.

Taxation

As far as taxation is concerned, generally income tax is lower than in the UK but you need to study the double-taxation regulations to see how these affect you. There are arrangements between the UK and several countries on these, and the general basis is a payment of tax in both countries, although the amount in each case is less. For details, contact the Overseas Territories Income Tax Office in London. Also there is the question of indirect taxation, and this can make your cost of living zoom up, particularly when you need anything that is imported. This is where your regular stream of visitors can come in handy, if you brief them about your shortages and they take advantage, in their turn, of things which are cheaper to buy locally.

Other Costs
Car taxation varies considerably from country to country, as each has its own system. On the whole, car insurance rates tend to be higher than in the UK but petrol tends to cost about the same. Public transport spans a wide range from acutely uncomfortable to near luxury, and is usually cheaper. There are some obvious bonuses: house-heating needs to be on for a much shorter period and decoration and repairs can be done at lower rates, while electricity, gas and water cost less.

But, taking it overall, the total you will spend will not be a lot different than if you had stayed at home. The difference is what you spend it on. If you enjoy eating out, that can often cost less in proportion than in the UK. If your drink is Scotch then the opposite usually applies. Clothes can be less formal if in a village or coastal area but, again, a cosy pullover, needed for chilly evenings, may be expensive or even unobtainable.

Pensions
The State pension is payable in all EEC countries, together with any increases in it which are approved from time to time. (The DHSS will give you the appropriate leaflet for the country of your choice.) This also applies to widows' pensions and allowances and war pensions, but *not* to supplementary benefits. Contact the Overseas Group of the DHSS at the address listed. Also, if retiring abroad before the usual ages of 65 and 60, you will not, of course, receive your pensions when reaching those ages.

MEDICAL CARE
Medical care can be a lot more expensive, so membership of such organisations as the British United Provident Association (BUPA) is desirable. If you are already a member you can take out an extension of your policy for overseas cover. It is always a wise idea to have a very thorough health check before deciding to live abroad, as if you go down with something really serious, there is the psychological effect of difficulty in communication to add to feeling terribly ill. For those who have not become permanently resident abroad, the National Health

Service treatment in the UK is available, but this must be weighed against the need for both you and your spouse to be able to stay in the UK during the hospital or other treatment. That can push up costs unless there are family or friends to provide a room for the husband or wife who accompanies the patient. There are, as always, forms to be signed before you can be sure of full cover, even with EEC countries, and plenty of time must be allowed for these to move along the pipeline. We have known people all ready to move into their new home, who have had to spend another couple of months in the UK waiting for the slow march of bureaucracy.

BUYING PROPERTY

Property can be bought on mortgage through the bank, or there are stage payments where the balance is spread over a stated number of years, following the initial deposit. Where to buy? It is wise to avoid the construction of a purpose-built home, supervised by you at a long distance without knowledge of the language. The Overseas Property Guide, an annual publication, contains a great deal of information about properties in all the popular and many less well-known retirement areas.

Residents' permits also have to be obtained in certain cases – e.g. the south coast of France – or application for permanent residence after a stay of 90 days has to be made if you decide to reside in Spain.

Whether or not to take all your own furniture has to be weighed up carefully, because of the import-tax and duty procedures which can be very complicated. If the furniture/furnishings are not worth a lot, it is probably cheaper and easier to re-furnish on the spot. However, some friends of ours with a house full of antiques and near-antiques were strongly advised to take these with them to France because prices for British antiques were very favourable in that country. In such cases, it is essential to go to a firm of removers with long experience of this type of work. The British Association of Removers issue a leaflet on overseas removals, full of handy hints and a check list. Another leaflet, produced by Pickfords, gives plenty of good advice to those settling in Spain, where more than 22,000 retired British people now live. This touches on such matters as *residencias*, importation of cars, taking your pets and the type of electrical voltage obtaining in the area chosen. Fincasol, overseas agents, warn that it can take at least 6 months to adjust to the different style of living and that, before making the move, it is essential to learn at least something of the language.

More information is available from the monthly magazine *Homes*

Overseas, obtainable at larger newsagents, and a book *Buying Property Overseas*, published by the same magazine, which also operates a readers' enquiry service.

You can avoid problems by finding out about all those extra costs which have to be paid on top of the purchase price. In a community development there are maintenance charges as well as the local property taxes and, in Spain, these can mount up to several hundred pounds a year. In France there is VAT to be paid, as well as regional and real-estate taxes. If buying a newly-built villa in Spain you may be required to make stage payments and, when contracts have been exchanged, there are the notary's fees, together with transfer and value tax. As when buying in the UK, it is always advisable to have your own solicitor, as the notary is a public official who acts for both buyer and seller, so does not exclusively represent your interests.

There are countries, such as Greece, where unless you are a national you are not allowed to buy property, so if you opt for living there it will be a question of renting.

LIVING ABROAD

Politics? The best advice with regard to getting involved in local politics is 'don't'. Apart from being intrusive and discourteous, it is bound to cause trouble, as it takes a long time to know who is linked with whom because inter-relations can be extremely complex. Unless you are an expert on the country of your choice, the best policy is to observe but not criticise.

Finally, a cautionary word, whether you decide to stay put in the UK or move abroad in search of sunshine. At all costs, avoid the 'ghetto mentality'. Try to integrate into the community as a whole, instead of segregating yourself into a narrow world consisting of no one under 60. All age groups need to learn from the others and you are going to get very little cross-fertilisation of ideas if you mix solely with people whose experiences are exactly the same as your own. When you were working or bringing up a family you had to get on with people of all ages. Now that you are coming up to retirement there is a need for the same process to go on if you are to be mentally stimulated and to enjoy life to the full.

6 TRANSPORT

It is very difficult to budget accurately for many of the expenses in running a home, especially for food, toiletries and replacement of furniture, curtains and bed-linen. One item which can be costed quite precisely is the car. In looking at your finances before retirement day, you can work out just what it costs you and decide whether it should be retained or could be replaced by a smaller and cheaper model, or even dispensed with completely so that you hire a car when needed or use public transport.

YOUR CAR

If you have a company car, it may be possible to buy this from your firm. This could be a way of reducing costs if you are a two-car household. By selling your own vehicle you could free cash to pay for the firm's car with which you are equally familiar. When neither is used in connection with a business there is far less need for two cars. There is no longer any need to ferry the children around, because by now they should have left home or, if still under your roof, should have their own transport. If that is not so, it might be worthwhile sorting out a car-sharing arrangement, but the terms would have to be clearly spelt out and enforced or you might end up with very little use of the car for yourself while picking up all the bills.

There are two sound arguments for retaining one or both cars in certain circumstances. The first is if you intend to obtain another job and the other is if you opt for self-employment. In the former case, the ability to drive is generally taken for granted and if the firm do not provide company cars then they are looking for someone with his or her own transport. In the second case you will be under a disadvantage if you have to rely on hiring or on public transport, if the type of self-employment you have chosen involves any type of travel. There is also the point that you may want to use your car to make some extra money. Mini-cab services which offer a 24-hour coverage are always looking out for drivers. Generally the arrangement is based on a contribution to the cost of radio communication with the office, drivers making their profit out of charging the going rate for journeys, less the cost of petrol and the increased maintenance needed. Different firms have varying arrangements about the number of days worked per week and the length of shifts, so it is worth checking with several before you commit yourself.

If one car is paying for itself in this way, or is essential to your self-employment, there could be a reason for remaining a two-car household. The second car may be a smaller and cheaper model, but it would provide the convenience for shopping, visiting family and friends or for short distance holidays. If one of you is engaged in any voluntary work, such as meals-on-wheels, transport to and from hospitals, or taking elderly people out to clubs or day centres, this would also justify keeping a second car.

If you really enjoy driving and, even more, if you enjoy doing much of your own servicing, it would be a great pity to get rid of your car just because it represents a large chunk of your expenses. It would be better to look around at other directions in which you can save, should that be necessary. Quite a few people would rather sell their home and buy a smaller one, or stay where they are and add to their income by holiday lettings, than get rid of their car. If that is how you feel, then by all means keep it. But you will need to be realistic about the annual cost. By doing most of your repairs and by regular maintenance it is possible that you will not spend much more than you would on any other hobby you take up in retirement. Your car would become your hobby and could be costed on that basis.

If your choice of holiday is camping, then you will certainly want to keep the car, whether you travel from one camping site to another or have invested in your own caravan. The special thing about holidays of this type is that time limits no longer matter. You do not have to return from a holiday just at peak of enjoyment simply because you have to be in the office on Monday morning. You can go further afield and stay longer if you have no business ties.

Another point is that, instead of sitting snarling at yourself in traffic jams, you can set out and return at the least busy times.

FITNESS TO DRIVE

Fitness to drive is a point which often comes up in discussion. Provided that an older driver is generally physically fit he is usually less likely to get into an accident than a younger one who is less experienced and more inclined to drive too fast. Insurance companies are not in the charity business, yet some of the larger ones offer very attractive terms specifically for the more mature driver. Sun Alliance claim that their 'Motorist 50+' policy is the first of its kind. Drivers are eligible if aged 50 or over, with at least 3-years' no-claim discount, and if they are driving a family saloon or estate car with low annual mileage. The cover is limited to the owner-driver and any two other careful drivers aged 50 or over, nominated by him or her. The only person under 50 who can drive the car is the wife or husband, provided they are more than 35 years of age.

While it is true that reactions may become slower as you grow older, this is not always so and, in any case, it can be offset by experience. The indecisive driver may be 18 or 80, and some of the worst driving can be found among people who have just passed their test and who think that all learning stops there.

The advice in Chapter 1 mentioned regular check-ups. This is obviously important if you intend to carry on driving as long as possible. If you feel that your long-distance vision is not what it was, ask the optician's opinion about driving. Another point to watch is this. If prescribed any medicines with which you are not familiar, check with the doctor or pharmacist whether these have a slowing-down effect. The doctor may mention this when prescribing, but do not count on it, and if buying over the counter at the chemist it is advisable to ask about this and to read all the instructions. Quite a number offer cautions against driving or using machinery while taking the medication.

PUBLIC TRANSPORT

Whether or not you decide to keep your car or cars, there must be many occasions when it is preferable to use public transport. It might be when shopping in a big city where parking can be a nightmare, or nipping up to your local centre for a few things which have been overlooked in the main weekly shopping expedition. Full information on the age concessions which apply to public transport can be obtained from any travel agent. Within the Greater London area there are bus passes which also cover travelling on the underground. If you are active and like to get about, these can represent a very considerable saving over a year. The only restriction is that they cannot be used before half past nine in the morning, but after that the travel is absolutely free. Application forms for the passes are obtainable from post offices and a refund is made for the cost of two passport-type photographs which can be obtained from one of the do-it-yourself kiosks to be found in many department stores and at a number of railway stations.

Another concession is the half-price travel on main line and suburban railways. This applies to anyone over 60 years of age in any part of the UK. The travel cards are bought annually and the current payment for a Senior Citizen Railcard is £12 (1985), with a cheaper card (£7) for a slightly more restricted concession. Reductions of one-half on some tickets and one-third on others can quickly pay for the initial outlay and, if you decide you want to have the benefit of the full (£12) card, having bought the lower-priced one, you can pay the difference at any time. There is also a Rail Europ card sponsored by European railways, for men aged 65 and over and women aged 60 and over. Currently this costs £5 and provides discounts on rail travel in Europe and reductions on shipping services to the Channel Islands and the Irish ports, as well as through-travel to Dublin City centre.

Incentive travel often takes the form of coupons which can be collected from household items. These offer subsidised travel on British Rail, usually with one person paying a fare and one or more going free or at a very reduced level. As children generally go free, this is an excellent way of organising a family outing for three generations.

Even if you never get around to collecting coupons, there are travel concessions which can be obtained if sufficient number of people get together to fill a carriage. It is also possible to hire a minibus (self-drive or with driver) to pick you all up at the other end. You can then either go around together or disperse and meet up at a collecting point at the end of the day.

CAR-SHARING

As time goes on, it is possible that health problems may cause you to give up driving. This could be so if arthritis makes steering difficult or if there are problems regarding eyesight. For very many people even these difficulties can be overcome, but one must recognise that this is not always the case. There is also the fact that, particularly after an illness, a driver may find it too tiring to cope with motorway traffic or the hassle of finding parking space.

Even so, these problems are not insuperable. This is the time to consider car-sharing. A friend of ours has an arrangement with an old buddy to do just that. He pays for licensing and insuring the car and his friend acts as chauffeur for his shopping expeditions, collects his visitors from the railway station and also ferries him to doctor's and dentist's surgeries. Because they get on well together, this works very smoothly and it is easy to sort out alternative arrangements when the driver wants to go off on holiday.

If you have decided to give up your car but still own a garage, you can let it either for someone else's vehicle or for furniture storage, and the money can go towards other household expenses. Alternatively, you may have a hobby for which space is needed and the garage can then become a very useful workshop.

SERVICING YOUR CAR

You may never have carried out any servicing on your car. Now is the time to get some idea of how the car operates. It is possible that you have never read the handbook. If so, do it now and carry out the weekly routine which it advises. This will include checking that the radiator and battery are topped up with water (distilled water in the latter case). You will also need to check tyre pressure and oil level. You will need to look over the tyres to see if there is any obvious wear or damage and that the dust caps are properly in place. There are very good classes on car maintenance at local adult-education centres and you might well enrol in one of these before retirement date. These classes attract as many women as men, and it can be a money-saver if you do not have to leave every minor problem to the garage. Garages have a way of making the most minor repair into a major one. Some women are very good mechanics. That was shown during World War 2 when plenty of girls took standard and advanced training in maintaining and driving vehicles of all types. Many were running and repairing heavy lorries. Queen Elizabeth II was one of those who enrolled at 18 years of age, and learned to drive and maintain six-wheelers. Present-day cars do not present the same problems as army lorries of the 1940s, and the present tendency is to replace rather than repair, but it is still useful to be wised up on the basics. There is the incentive to save money when retirement is on the horizon and to get the maximum value out of your car.

While you have been earning, assuming you do not do your own servicing, it is probable that you have had a regular servicing arrangement. Unless you become skilled in that direction, it is a worthwhile expense to continue this and also to trade in the car for a newer model every other year or so.

We are also assuming that you are a member of either the Automobile Association or the Royal Automobile Club and take full advantage of their services. However, you will not want to call on these if you can spot some of the simpler troubles yourself. Many of them are connected with the vehicle's needs for water, oil or petrol, or with carelessness in connecting leads, replacing dust caps or radiator caps, or omitting to check the state of the battery.

OTHER FORMS OF TRANSPORT

Suppose you decide to sell your car and to look for some other form of secondary transport? It might be a moped for minor shopping jaunts, which is both handy and inexpensive, or it could be a bicycle, which has the advantage of providing healthy exercise as well. If you learned to ride a bike when a child you will be amazed at how quickly you get used to it again. In a busy traffic area you may prefer to confine your trips to side-roads, to begin with, until you get used to coping with main roads.

7 SAFETY IN THE HOME

Safety precautions are not something that applies only to small children or to very old people. Whatever your age, you need to watch out for hazards such as the trailing flex, the slippery floor or the badly-lit stairs. Or, better still, anticipate trouble and do something about it before you or other people have an accident

AVOIDING ACCIDENTS

It is often said that the home must be a very dangerous place because that is where so many accidents occur. To some extent the place of work is likely to be safer because of statutory regulations but, even there, if someone can take a short cut through the procedures, or leave off a guard on a machine to speed up his output, he almost certainly will.

Even familiarity with the risks does not act as a deterrent. An insurance official told us about three claims he found on his desk last week. The first was from a man who fell and broke his arm because his mate, pruning the same tree, sawed through the branch on which this chap was sitting. The second was from a window-cleaner who stepped out into thin air because another man had borrowed his ladder for a moment and forgotten to tell him. The third – our favourite – was the workman, who removed a manhole cover, wandered around trying to find somewhere to put it, fell back into the manhole and pulled the cover down on top!

So we are all vulnerable, but some are more vulnerable than others. As you get older, you gradually begin to move and react more slowly and to lose your balance more easily. In addition, distance sight tends to be less efficient and, for those who have to wear bifocals it is necessary to gauge different levels more carefully.

Well before retirement age, it is worthwhile to make a survey of the house, garden and garage and tighten up on anything likely to become a hazard. Often only a minor repair is involved, or even just a change of working habits. But if any expense does become necessary, it is easier to deal with it while still earning rather than to wait until you have only your pension. Recently, the Royal Society for the Prevention of Accidents and Age Concern launched a campaign 'Safety in Retirement', which admirably summed up all the points that need to be watched in or around the home. These apply not only to pensioners but to people of all ages. The only difference is that the serious accident percentages seem to rise noticeably after the age of 65 and very much more from 75. The need to make sure that doorways, landings, halls and stairs are free from clutter and well-lit is stressed. If there is no bedside lamp or switch within easy reach, then a torch should be kept by the bed. There should be a hand-rail at each side of the stairs, one by the toilet and another by the bath. Windows and doors in all rooms should open and shut easily. A rubber mat in the bath helps people to keep their balance. Floors and floorcoverings should not be uneven or slippery and any spillages need to be cleaned up immediately. Most importantly, there should be no trailing flexes in any area.

Bending down or climbing up can involve accidents with elderly people. So, even if you're only 50, when you are planning for retirement it saves time and money if you do it as if for someone much older – then you will not need to do it again in 20 years time when you will have less energy and probably less cash.

Never climb up on a chair or table when changing a light bulb, and this applies even more when changing a fluorescent tube. Have a stepladder for the job and always remember to switch off the light before taking out the old bulb or tube. If you are fitting a new front door, have a letter box with a back on it. Then you will not have to stoop to pick up the post and papers from the mat. A shelf at waist height outside the door is a better place for milk bottles than ground level, as again it cuts out stooping. Take a good look at your fitted cupboards, especially in the kitchen. There is a tendency to put heavy items at the top, especially if they are used infrequently. It is better to store these at the back of a lower cupboard.

It is said that, as people get older, they use living room and bedroom more and spend less time in the kitchen. For that reason, unnecessary items of furniture should be got rid of in the two most-used rooms, so that there is a clear path for movement, without risk of knocking over extra chairs or occasional tables. The bedside is particularly important. If there is a chair near the bed, the seat of this should be the same height as the mattress; ideally it should be lightweight, with smooth running castors, so that it can be pushed out of the way if necessary. A bedside table should be no higher than the pillows. If you have to reach up to it, there is always the chance of spillages. Never drape a cloth over a table lamp. If the light is too bright, fit a bulb of lower wattage.

FIRE RISKS

The furniture arrangements in both rooms should not create a fire risk and, in addition, mirrors should never be hung over the fireplace, or bills and letters kept up there. An even level of warmth is advisable and the rooms should be free from draughts but, at the same time, well ventilated. Regular servicing of heaters of all types, plus regular cleaning of chimneys and flues is essential.

Scalds and burns can be a risk in the kitchen, whatever the fuel used. There is also the risk of fire, especially with chip pans. Cooking oils and fats can heat up to a point where they catch fire spontaneously, so it is best never to have the pan more than half full of oil. It may be difficult to remember, if the doorbell rings, but a chip pan should be taken off the heat even if left only for a minute.

Two other fire risks are the habit of drying tea-towels on the plate-rack over the hob, and storing a pile of newspapers in the space between cooker and wall. Both are just asking for trouble. Another is when wooden pan handles are left across a lighted burner: it is often done to save turning the burner out while dishing up from other pans. Just as risky is positioning the pans with the handles facing out into the kitchen. Here it is a risk of scalding as you brush past rather than of anything catching fire.

If you have an electric kettle on the worktop beside the cooker, always watch that the flex does not trail across the hob, and always unplug it before filling or pouring. It is not the best place for the kettle, but there may not be room for it anywhere else. With gas cookers, keep an eye on pilot lights. Sudden gusts through the door or an adjoining window can easily blow these out. It is never wise to block up ventilators in a kitchen when you cook with gas, as appliances must have some fresh air if they are to burn properly. If you are redecorating the kitchen, remember that expanded-polystyrene ceiling tiles should not be painted with gloss or any other oil-based paints, as these encourage fire to spread quickly.

Emulsion paint is the right choice for this job. It goes without saying that, in the event of a power failure, it is necessary to switch off kettles, irons and other appliances, as well as radiant fires, because the power could come on again when you are not at home. If gas has to be turned off for any reason, turn off appliances and pilot lights first before turning off the main gas supply. When you turn on the main supply again, relight all the pilot lights on all the appliances.

If you are rewiring or planning an update of your wiring system, have a realistic look at the number of appliances you normally use. It does not cost much more to have a twin socket at quite a few locations. This is better than relying on adaptors, with the risk over overloading power points which were never intended to take a festoon of plugs. Also, do not use lighting points for appliances that need power points. It may be convenient to plug in the iron to a point designed to take a bedside light, but it will fuse it.

In the bedroom, risks can come through carelessness over electric blankets or hot-water bottles. Under-blankets should always be unplugged before getting into bed. *Some* over-blankets are designed for all night use, but make sure yours is one of these. If not, switch off and unplug. All electric blankets should be kept flat and be regularly serviced, as well as being kept dry. It is easy to check on the state of hot-water bottles. As they get older they can develop pinpoint holes or the screwtop can become badly fitting. Hold them over the sink and have a look at them closely to see if they are watertight, give them a slight shake and turn them upside down to see if there is any leakage from the top.

Before leaving fire risks, let us look at one of the chief culprits – smoking. The minimum precaution to take is to have plenty of deep ashtrays, and to be sure that you and other people use them. We have often seen lighted cigarettes left on the edge of a chimney piece or the side of a bath or basin. Use wastepaper bins rather than baskets – plenty of hot cigarette ends or not-quite-spent matches get thrown into the latter, with sensational results, or pipes with glowing embers knocked out into them. Smoking in bed is a real culprit when it comes to fires. More than a thousand fires a year result from this and many of these have been very serious indeed. This is more the fault of middle-aged people rather than the elderly, and the only thing to be done, if it is a persistent habit, is to make sure that there is a heavy, deep glass ashtray near the bed. Smoke alarms are not expensive and are well worth installing near areas of risk, such as kitchens, lounges and smoker's bedrooms.

AVOIDING FALLS

The RoSPA/Age Concern campaign includes a very helpful leaflet for the elderly on avoiding falls, not only by improving the environment in the home, but also by taking safety precautions. Among tips they offer are sitting upright on a straight-backed chair when dressing; coming down stairs one step at a time and counting steps as you go or, if it feels safer, coming down backwards; making sure that all spillages are wiped up immediately; gripping something secure when reaching up to a high shelf or bending down to a low cupboard.

FIRST AID

In the kitchen, one of the most useful gadgets is an efficient wall can-opener. Plenty of cuts come from gashes made by hand-held openers, which may be too blunt for the can but are still able to give a very nasty gash. There should be a first-aid box near the kitchen as well as one in the bathroom. If the kitchen is dry, well ventilated and not overheated, it is a suitable place also for the medicine cupboard, kept well away from foodstuffs, preferably among the china and glass. Many medicines need to be taken with water, or be diluted, so it is a logical place to have them. Never take medicine prescribed for anyone else. Keep all medicines in their original containers, and take them only at the times and in the doses prescribed. Finish the supply given – doctors say that half their patients stop taking the tablets as soon as they begin to feel a bit better but before the trouble has really cleared up. If it is necessary to have any left-overs, flush these away or hand them into the pharmacist to be destroyed.

DO-IT-YOURSELF EQUIPMENT

The elderly are not so likely to engage in active do-it-yourself or gardening, but the middle-aged, coming up to retirement, certainly are. Mowers, garden tools and do-it-yourself equipment are common sources of cuts and shocks. Again, do not take chances. If anything you are using is at all suspect, put it right – if you know how – or get it serviced instead of postponing it.

Coming up to retirement is a time to review all DIY equipment, to get repairs done to any items, to stock up on spare parts you know will be needed later and buy labour-saving tools which you have been needing for a long time but never got around to purchasing. Some of these could be birthday or Christmas presents and others could be budgeted for in the years before actual retirement.

One of the most useful items we bought was a pair of lightweight steps. Lugging a very heavy pair around for years was energy-consuming and frayed the temper. Like most people we had far too much stored in inaccessible cupboards. That can be solved by re-arranging the contents of the cupboards or, where this is not possible, using the lightweight steps or a step-stool with a vertical grab pole. A lot of DIY cupboards are put in by husbands for their wives; a useful point to remember is that the average wife is 4 inches shorter than her husband and upper cupboards which he can reach easily are just too high for her.

It is not realistic to make pious resolutions about putting tools in racks and clearing up and tidying everything away at the end of the day. In nine cases out of ten this does not happen. But we have noticed that, when we have any jobs done by competent men, if they had to come back to continue the work next day, they always left all the clutter in one place, where it could be clearly seen, with anything sharp-edged safely at the back of the pile and with heavy implements that might take a burglar's fancy well hidden underneath. Upstairs it would usually be under a bed and, downstairs, behind or under a settee where no one could stumble over it in the dark.

COURSES

Handy courses are run by the Electricity Council. A woman who knows how to change a plug, replace a fluorescent tube or whether or not it is really necessary to call in an electrician when an appliance goes wrong, is less dependent on help from friends or neighbours. After all, none of these should be difficult to learn when someone has mastered an electric typewriter or word processor at the office, operated a complicated cash register or enjoyed the use of the video recorder at home, without even thinking about it.

GAS APPLIANCES

Gas is as safe a fuel as any other. But like all fuels it needs to be used wisely. There are specific regulations about the use of gas. These lay down that nobody shall use – or let anybody else use – any gas appliance known or suspected to be dangerous; only competent people shall instal or service gas supplies, appliances or flues; you must turn off the main gas supply if a gas escape is suspected; you must tell the local Gas Service Centre at once if an escape continues after the main supply is turned off; you must not turn on the gas, or any appliance, again until the escape or the appliance has been repaired. These are strict points of law and can involve fines of up to as much as £2,000.

But, as with all fuels, accidents can happen. High on the list of causes are amateur DIY efforts at maintenance work or installation, or calling in a cowboy who has no experience of gas. So it is essential to get any work done either by the Gas Service Centre locally or by an independent CORGI-registered installer. (CORGI stands for Confederation for Registration of Gas Installers.)

Gas appliances need to breathe and may require a flue or chimney so that fumes from the appliance are not mixed with the fresh air you need to breathe. For that reason it is essential to ensure that the chimney is swept before any gas heater is installed. Others, such as the balanced-flue or room-sealed appliances, use a system which seals off both the ventilation and flueing from the room. They take fresh air directly from the exterior of the house and discharge their fumes outside. We have noticed with this type of heater that there is never any stuffiness in the room, however much the appliance is used. The only point to watch in deciding to instal this sort of heater is that the outside grille should never be blocked up or have anything resting against it. So if you have neighbours who are prone to pile stuff against the wall where you plan to have such a heater, think again about whether you can position it in a different place.

Water heaters also use the balanced-flue system and, for some years, it has been illegal to instal any except balanced-flue water heaters in bathrooms. All the same, there are many older models using ordinary flues which still work very well and, if you have one of this type, it is important to follow some simple safety rules.

1. First, make sure the room is well ventilated and that the flue system above it is in good repair.
2. Always open the bathroom door or window when drawing off hot water.
3. Turn off the water heater before getting into the bath.
4. Do not run more hot water while in the bath.
5. Keep bathroom ventilators free from obstruction.
6. Have the water heater serviced at least once a year.

If you have an unflued instantaneous sink heater, you should not run it continuously for a period longer than 5 minutes, and this type of heater is not designed for filling washing machines or for showers. Like all forms of gas central heating and fires, water heaters should be serviced at least once a year, while a check every 2 years should be sufficient for other gas apparatus. It pays to take advantage of the special offers for servicing, which include checking the flues.

Anyone over the age of 65, who lives alone, and any registered disabled person of any age who lives alone, is entitled to a free safety check on gas appliances and installations. This check covers a small sum (not charged to the householder) for any adjustments and materials needed. If any further work is required, you will have to pay for it, but you will be given an official estimate showing what this comes to and, in a number of cases, you may be able to get help towards the cost from the local Social Security Office or Social Services Department. So, find out if you are entitled to any help before you agree to any extra work being done. You can arrange for this check via the showroom or service centre (see phone number under GAS in local directory).

If you have a disability which makes it hard to operate a gas appliance, special controls and adaptors can be provided at a very low charge for each appliance, and some cookers, fires and central heating units can also be fitted with Braille controls. Again, with gas meters, you may have problems in operating the coin meter and, in this case, an attachment handle can be supplied free of charge or you can change, again with no charge, to a credit meter. If you experience difficulty in reaching the gas meter, it can be moved to a more convenient position. The charge is very low if the new position is within 3 feet of the present one, but a quotation would have to be given, and the cost would be more, if it had to be moved further away. A further precaution: British Gas advise turning off the main supply when you go on holiday. Should there be any smell of gas when it is turned on again, notify them immediately.

RADIANT HEATING

Whatever the fuel, where there are elderly or infirm people, it is advisable to err on the side of caution as regards any form of radiant heating. Both modern gas and electric fires incorporate dress guards, but for older people a surrounding guard is advisable in addition. Suitable guards cover the whole area around the fire and not just the fire-front. The nursery guard, used with a solid-fuel fire, can still allow, by means of a hinged flap, for adding fuel while it is in place. The cabinet-type guard for portable heaters gives the extra protection needed. As an additional precaution in the case of portable gas or paraffin heaters, ensure that they are not in a draught and are kept away from chairs, curtains and other furnishings. Any form of portable heater requires extra care and such heaters are not an ideal choice for people who are unsteady on their feet or suffer from any other disability. Most of the precautions needed are no more than commonsense, e.g. you should never take a portable mains-operated electric heater into the bathroom. A spark guard is needed for an open coal fire and should always be left in place when you go to bed at night.

If you use paraffin oil heaters or bottled gas, take even more care. Paraffin should always be stored in a safe place, away from heat and direct sunlight, and in proper conditions. Filling up with paraffin should not be done indoors, nor should any heater of this type be carried once it has been lit.

Many people use cylinder gas in caravans and mobile homes as well as in houses. As always, plenty of ventilation is essential. If vents have been built into caravans or mobile homes, they must never be blocked up or altered in any way. Even those pieces of apparatus which do not need a flue, such as cookers, portable heaters etc., still need plenty of air, as do fixed-flue appliances such as some water-heaters. All appliances should be regularly checked. If buying any apparatus running off bottled gas, avoid getting it second-hand: it pays to go to a shop selling new appliances with the BSI safety mark on them. Get it installed by an expert and have it regularly serviced. Store the cylinders in a safe place and, if doubtful on any of these points, ask advice of the supplier of the gas who can be found under 'Bottled gas suppliers' in Yellow Pages.

OUTSIDE THE HOUSE

Having dealt with the inside of the house, if planning for a safe retirement, take a look at the surrounds to your home. Tackle the concrete area between the back door and garden, which may be uneven and likely to cause someone to trip. Have a look at fences and gates to check that they are in a good state of repair. Nails tend to work loose with time and, if not the galvanised type, they will be rusty, so are best hammered in or, preferably, replaced. The dustbin should be sited as close as possible to the kitchen door. If yours is in a fixed type of bunker, then it should be planned so that it is only a few feet away from the house. If you put a black plastic bag inside the bin, you can leave out the bag for collection. The bin will last much longer that way.

There should be safe lighting in the garage and any shed that is used as a workshop, with the right type of power points for using electrical equipment there and also for outdoor appliances, such as mowers and hedge-trimmers. Even when there is no shed or garage, it is a useful idea to fit a bulkhead light to the outside of the house, switched from inside the house, to light your way if you have to go into the garden after dark.

It is good neighbourliness to site it so that it illuminates your garden only, and does not shine into the windows of any adjoining house. If you are contemplating buying a greenhouse or cold frame, consider one with plastic panels instead of glass. They are safer if you have grandchildren or animals playing in the garden.

RUBBISH DISPOSAL

If you live in an area where bonfires are permitted, try to keep the number as low as possible. The first fine day, with everyone's windows open, seems to act as a magnet to compulsive bonfire-setters, just as it does to those with powerful amplifiers. Wood smoke can be pleasant in moderation, but the same cannot be said for piles of damp weeds, mounds of paper or unwanted three piece suites. In the latter case, it is worth remembering that it is illegal to burn synthetic materials which give off toxic fumes. If you have all that amount, hire a skip. If there is less, then either a mini-skip at half the cost could be the answer, or you can find the nearest dump and take the refuse up there yourself or persuade a friend to do it for you. The weekend is the right time, as it is generally free.

GARDENING

Do not strain to move heavy materials in the garden without suitable equipment. There are plenty of rugged trolleys which take the back-breaking work out of it and, if space is too limited for a conventional wheelbarrow, there are the newer fold-up kinds.

When choosing new garden tools, keep an eye open for those which take the hard work out of digging and planting. Long-handled trowels enable you to reach the back of the rockery without difficulty. Spades and forks do not need to weigh a ton to do their job efficiently: if a garden tool is too heavy to use it is going to end up unused.

One problem for gardeners as they get older is that kneeling on paths and flowerbeds, or even on grass, can become painful very quickly. A very useful buy is a plastic-covered foam mat, which can be used outdoors as well as inside the house. Alternatively, there are metal-framed seats which can be turned over so that the seat area becomes a kneeler when required. These have the added advantage, if getting up is difficult, of allowing you to lever yourself upright by hanging on to the frame.

STEPS
Every time there is ice or snow, steps leading to a front door can become a real hazard. Our own short flight was especially risky because there was no hand-rail at either side. That was the first thing to be rectified and, more recently, it has been planned to replace the steps with a ramp.

8 HOME AND PERSONAL SECURITY

Earlier on, we mentioned avoiding the ghetto mentality. An equally unwise attitude to beware of is the siege mentality. Many retired or elderly people seem to fasten on every break-in or mugging reported in the local press, so that in listening to them one can get the false impression that this is something happening to everyone in the area.

This is not intended to play down the number of larcenies or personal attacks. But you will notice that those involving older age groups always receive prominence in the media, while there is little reference to younger people. Yet in fact there are far more attacks on young men – much more than on young women and elderly pensioners – and many of these are very serious indeed.

So do not let other people's nervousness infect you and make you a prisoner in your own home. Instead, take a positive approach and find out all you can about two points:
1. How to make your home and other possessions as secure as possible.
2. How to defend yourself.

MAKING YOUR HOME SECURE
We went to the Crime Prevention Officer in our area of London and here is some of the practical advice that was given.

Tackle the front door first. Fit a door chain, but make sure that the door is strong enough to take it and that the screws are sufficiently long to do the job. It should be impossible to take off the chain unless the door is fully closed. Mortise locks are essential and two are better than one. There should be a bolt about one-third down from the top of the door and another about one-third up from the bottom of it. If you have a letter-flap, then fit a box or cage at the back of it. This not only saves bending down to pick up the mail, but also guards against someone reaching through the flap to try to withdraw a bolt or reach a lock on the inside.

Fit a spy-hole, but take the precaution of having a light above it. It is a waste of time looking through it into complete darkness – you should be able to see the person standing outside. If you have trees or shrubs shading the front door, keep these cut back sufficiently to enable you to see callers. This will also deter anyone from breaking in through the door as they will be visible from the pavement or road. A bulkhead fitting over the garage is another practical idea, plus another which illuminates the garden – both switched on from inside the house.

Being security-minded means that you take a realistic view of risks and do everything possible to protect your home. It does not mean complication, disproportionate expense or living in a constant state of fear. You may have a single room, a flat, or your home may be a detached house or bungalow with garden, garage and shed. If it is a furnished room, fit the strongest lock consistent with the strength of the door, if the landlord has not already made suitable provision. When at home, keep a chain on the door and leave it on until you recognise your visitors. Whether you will also need window locks depends on the exterior of the building, e.g. the presence of a fire escape and whether downpipes are accessible to the window, offering a foothold to an enterprising burglar.

In the case of a flat, its security will be affected by whether it is a ground-floor flat or one on the upper floors. The former is more vulnerable and all windows and doors will need efficient locks. The upper-floor flat comes in the same category as the furnished room, with the need not only for protection against break-ins from outside but also by other occupants of the building. Nowadays a mansion-style flat generally has a doorkeeper and often an entry-phone system as well as extra forms of security.

When it comes to a house, the approach has to be more flexible, depending on whether it forms part of a terrace, is semi-detached or completely detached with access from four directions.

The first step is to ask at the nearest police station for a form 'Request for security survey' and to fill it in, stating when you are usually available. It helps the Crime Prevention Officer if he can come along in daylight because he can do a better survey of the premises, taking note of access routes from neighbouring gardens and how easy it may be to reach the upper floors. He is likely to spot points you may have overlooked because you do not think like a burglar, whereas his success depends on knowing how a crook's mind functions. He will recommend the types of lock you need for doors and windows and tell you whether a burglar alarm or panic button is required. If an alarm system is advisable it should be as simple as possible; if it is too complicated, people either neglect to use it or do so incorrectly. The police will probably suggest that you go to a firm which is a member of the NSCIA (National Supervisory Council for Intruder Alarms). The system may be a bit dearer than from a mail-order firm, but is likely to be more dependable. Also you can arrange a maintenance contract to keep it always in working order.

If a panic-button system is used, the box that is visible high up on the front of the house does not disclose if it is a full-scale alarm or a simple two-button system, so a burglar would have to break in before he could find out. One system which costs just under £100 at the present time has a button sited in the hall, a little way back from the front door. It is not placed right next to the front door because, if you open it, you could be pushed back as a thief forces his way in. This system is a fail-safe one, operating both on mains and batteries. A second panic button can also be fitted near to your bed.

It is advisable to tell the police that this has been installed, and to give them the name of any keyholder in the area – friend or relative. You should also warn your next-door neighbour, so that they can dial 999 immediately they hear the alarm go off.

Another point that the Crime Prevention Officer will stress is the need to treat back doors as seriously as front doors. There should be a mortise lock on the back door, as well as two bolts. It is good sense to choose the same type of mortise lock as on the front, so that keys match. Most areas have a locksmith who is a member of the Master Locksmiths Association, and it is best to ask him to fit any locks, rather than to go to a general handyman whom you may not know much about.

Garden sheds should always be kept locked. No one is likely to steal your spade or fork, but they would find it quite useful as a tool when breaking into the house. If the shed is long enough to take a single or sectional ladder, that is the best place for it. Should the ladder have to be kept outside, then it should be stowed away under cover and padlocked. One friend built a low double wall, with space in between for his ladder which rested on half-bricks to keep it off the wet concrete. A wooden lid, suitably weatherproofed, spanned the two low walls and this was used as a site for lightweight plastic troughs. When planted with geraniums, these gave a colourful display when viewed from the kitchen window nearby.

With regard to ladders, it is not only your own home that is put at risk if you leave them lying around. They are often taken to give access to your neighbours' homes, and you are not going to be popular in the street when they find out how the burglar managed to break in.

It goes without saying that a garage – whether integral or separate from the house – should have a strong lock. If it forms part of the house, the burglar-alarm system will need to apply to it as well.

Many people build a porch on to their homes to cut down draughts. Treat this as a first line of defence and lock it whenever you go out. Ready-made porches are available with letter-flaps, but if you build your own, remember to include this item. If the postman has to open the porch door to deliver the post, then anyone else can get inside and work quietly away on your front door. Passers-by take little notice of anyone inside a porch, as they assume that it is someone who belongs to the house.

One reason for obtaining advice from the Crime Prevention Officer rather than from friends or neighbours is that, if you go ahead on your own, you may incur expense on something which is not so suitable in your own case. For instance, he can advise on the best types of window lock for people who have arthritis in their hands or other disabilities.

Often there is a common passageway between two detached houses or a pair of semi-detached properties. It is worth finding out if your neighbour will agree to sharing the cost of a tall gate across it, level with the front of the two houses. This can be fitted with a strong lock, for which you both have a key. In this way, you create a double barrier – the front gate plus the individual back gates at the other end of the passage. This is a suitable arrangement when the passage is less than a car width, because it tends to be used infrequently, except for putting out refuse bins or providing access for repairs.

A strongly-growing rose is an effective deterrent when trained just above the top of the tall gate. Not many burglars like to tangle with a rose and among the most thorn-studded climbers and ramblers, well designed to repel them, are the following. Flammentanz is a very vigorous climber reaching to 20·feet high, with stems covered with large thorns. The flowers are scarlet and slightly fragrant, but will not smell good to a burglar. Paul's Scarlet Climber (actually a rambler) and New Dawn (another rambler) will go up to 13 feet and are reasonably thorny, as well as fragrant. New Dawn has flesh-pink double flowers. One of the best ramblers is *Rosa × Paulii*, which can be trained up to 20 feet and has large and small thorns which make it almost as inpenetrable as a bramble hedge.

Roses also make a no-go area in your garden if you train them as a hedge against a simple wire or chain-link fence. The white single-flowered *Rosa eglanteria*, compact though slow-growing, can also be used for hedging, as the stems are closely covered with small thorns. There is the bonus of colourful rose hips in the autumn. You can plan your security perimeters to be as floral and fragrant as you wish, with shrubs such as firethorn (*Pyracantha*), *Mahonia* and *Berberis*. One point to watch. Do not allow hedges to grow so tall that they obstruct your view and put your neighbour's plants in the shade. Do not let them grow forward so much that they provide useful dark corners for anyone lurking in the garden.

Break-ins have occurred because people have developed the bad habit of leaving a back-bedroom window slightly ajar so that the family cat can get in when it rains. Eventually a burglar has spotted this and copied the cat. It is better to fit a cat-flap on the ground floor. Most people fit cat-flaps to a rear door, but if fixed into the brickwork they are just as effective and there is no risk of weakening the door.

A bit of a bluff does not come amiss. You do not have to own a dog to put a 'Beware of the Dog' notice on your gate, especially one with a picture of an Alsatian.

When you do go out, leave on a radio with the volume turned up so that it can be heard by anyone just outside the front door. This can be a put-off for would-be thieves. Do not make it too loud, or your neighbours will curse you.

Some people fit an alarm box on the front of the house, up near the eaves, but in fact do not have an alarm to go with it. You may get away with it, but a pebble thrown up at it will make a hollow sound, giving the game away. So if you try this dodge, make sure there is something heavy in the box which will give a solid thud when hit by a stone. There is a good chance that the burglar will be deterred from breaking in. Better still – take the trouble to have a really efficient alarm fitted.

To sum up, ask the police to check out the vulnerable points in your home and follow their recommendations. Keep in touch with friends and neighbours, but do not make the mistake of locking yourself in so much that you cannot get out quickly in case of fire. Doors are the obvious exits for ground-floor escape from fire and windows for escape from upstairs. If there is a kitchen upstairs, it is advisable to keep a domestic fire extinguisher handy. These are easy to use and light to carry, but do not wait for a fire to find out how they work.

MARKING AND RECORDING YOUR POSSESSIONS

Thousands of viewers have watched programmes such as the *Antiques Roadshow* and seen how often people have been living for years with treasures, without any idea of their value. One family were even using a Ming vase for umbrellas.

You can take colour photographs of anything you believe to be valuable. Do this against a plain background and put a 1-foot ruler in front of the object to give an idea of scale. You should make a note of any lettering or other distinguishing marks which would not show up on the photograph. You can then send the picture for a professional valuation. You may be disappointed to find that your sideboard or painting has no value other than a sentimental one, but if it turns out to be quite pricey then you would do well to look at the level of your house contents insurance and find out if the premium needs to be raised.

Not long ago the Metropolitan Police brought out a scheme for marking objects by house number, or name and post-code, which must have caused plenty of chagrin among burglars. With this system you stand more chance of having your stolen property identified and returned to you, should it be recovered. There is the additional advantage that the thief will have less chance of selling at a favourable price, because an article with a code mark immediately becomes a hot property and will fetch a lower rate. The price of a video, for instance, can be halved when the buyer spots the mark.

The scheme provides for three types of marking. The first is punching, using a hammer and a set of punches bearing letters and figures. This is suitable for heavier goods, such as lawn-mowers, bicycles etc., but not for aluminium, which can easily be damaged. The second type of marking is by engraving, either freehand or using a stencil or template. Both these methods leave a permanent mark. This can be put in an unobtrusive place, and should be on a surface which cannot be removed without spoiling the appearance of the article or affecting its performance.

For cars there is a special window-etching kit that is also suitable for glassware, such as decanters and fruit bowls.

The third form of protection employs a pen containing ultra-violet ink. This is as simple to use as any ballpoint pen, remembering that unlike those pens it does not write when held upwards. This marking, unlike the other two types, is invisible but, if the article is stolen and later recovered, it can be identified by the police using an ultra-violet lamp. The pens cost between £1 and £2 each at most well-known stationers. There is a thick one, suitable for furniture, television sets and so on, and a thinner one for smaller articles, e.g. the base of a china vase. Being ultra-violet, the marking can fade and will need to be freshened up now and again. For furniture, make the mark on the back or underneath. If made on a surface that will be in the full sun, or one that is regularly polished, it will not last so long.

What happens if you move, or sell some of your belongings? All that is needed is to mark the pieces again, putting an 'X' at the end of the original code and entering the new code above it. It would be difficult for a thief to try to argue his way out of it, if caught, because the odds against him being able to prove he had lived at both addresses would be fantastic.

If pictures, china or furniture are very valuable, you should seek advice on where to put the mark, because you do not want to obliterate any distinctive features which are an indication of value.

If you do not know your post code, you can find it by looking at the back pages of the Thomson local directories or asking at the nearest post office.

If making a will and leaving specific pieces, remember to inform the solicitor that they are already post-coded, so that the new address can be substituted.

PROTECTING YOUR CAR

Next to the house, the car is usually the most expensive asset that most people possess and, if there is more than one car, the value involved becomes really high. The graphs for stolen cars and for thefts from cars both show an upward trend, and car thieves often get away with it – literally – because people make it easy for them.

There is a simple seven-point routine which can become second nature if you follow it regularly whenever you leave your car unattended.
1. Remove the ignition key and activate the steering lock.
2. Close all windows.
3. Have an alarm or immobiliser fitted, or extra locks.
4. Take your belongings with you, or put them well out of sight. Never leave vehicle documents in the car.
5. Lock all doors, the boot and the sun roof.
6. Try to park in a public place and avoid unlit parking areas at night. Bear in mind when parking during the day that the busy office area you have chosen may be totally deserted when you return late at night.
7. Always mark your car and its contents.
   The only exception to (2) is if you leave a dog in the car in warm

weather, when some ventilation is essential. The choice will be closing all windows and taking the dog with you, or fitting a grille over one window which is slightly open.

The car is the one thing that you do not mark with the post code, but you can mark the registration number on the glass. This is not intended as a protection against joy-riders, but against 'ringing' – where someone decides to replace your car for a beaten-up version of the same make which he already has. You can either buy an acid-etching kit, obtainable from bike-accessory shops and costing around £7, or, particularly if the car is an expensive model, you can invest around £300 in a professional sand-blasting job, having the registration number marked on all windows, alloy wheels and the hood.

It also helps to use the ultra-violet marker on the roof lining and this will need renewing every 6 months. The engraving tool can be used on other parts of the vehicle, e.g. under the boot, on the floor under the carpet. A marked card hidden inside the door panel is also useful identification. So, too, are the marked property stickers which act as a deterrent to the casual car thief.

Why lose expensive petrol to an opportunist? You can guard against this by a locking petrol cap and you can protect expensive wheels and tyres by locking wheel-nuts. Both forms of guard are cheap and effective.

You may have a boat or caravan in your driveway, and motor-bike and bicycles in the garage. All these can be appropriately marked to assist in identification.

NEIGHBOURHOOD WATCH

Another way to help beat burglary and vandalism is by joining a Neighbourhood Watch scheme. This does not impose any obligations or mean that you are taking over the job of the police. It just puts into an organised form what a lot of people have been doing for years – keeping an eye on each other's homes, reporting anything suspicious and letting the police know when they will be away on holiday and giving them the name of someone who will have a key in their absence.

Often the police start a watch scheme by canvassing in an area and arranging a meeting to let everyone know about it. Sometimes a private individual will take the initiative in setting up a scheme. If you want to do that, check first at the police station, as they may already have started work on the same stretch of road. In any case, they can give you a great deal of help in getting a scheme started.

The role of a member of a Neighbourhood Watch group is to be on the not all are men – the charming woman who asks to use your telephone, in their street or in their block of flats and to report these, to invite the Crime Prevention Officer to carry out a free security survey of their own home, to mark their property as already described, and to be involved, as a good neighbour, in anything which will help to prevent crime in their area.

The Metropolitan Police have produced a useful contact card, listing points to be looked for when giving a description of a person or vehicle. Even if you cannot spot all the points listed, be on the alert so that you can give a better description than 'medium height, medium build, medium colouring'.

The street co-ordinator for a group takes an active part in helping to recruit newcomers to the scheme, distributing literature and lending a hand with property marking. This can include borrowing a marking kit from the Crime Prevention Officer, or raising funds to buy a kit for the group (at present costing around £100) and recouping the outlay by lending it out, for a small charge, to other groups.

Although everyone living in the road will be invited to join, not all will, so accept that and do not pressure them. Most will join later when they see the benefits. If it is a very long street, it is customary to split it up into sections of, say, one-third.

When a whole street has been dealt with, a sign is erected to show criminals that it is a no-go area for burglary. There are already indications that the putting up of these signs acts as a strong deterrent.

One point which the police emphasise is that the scheme is not an invitation to people to take on criminals, but merely to be aware of what is going on, to let the police know immediately, if urgency is required, and also to notify them of anything which looks suspicious. They stress that it is not a job for busybodies – just for good neighbours.

COMMONSENSE PRECAUTIONS

A Government booklet *Protect your Home* is also a source of commonsense advice regarding security for your home and is based on the practical experience of police forces throughout the UK.

Give-away indications of an empty house are: a garage with the door wide open and no car inside, curtains and blinds closed all day, at all windows, notes by the front door, full milk bottles on the step and newspapers still in the letter box. At night, darkened rooms with the curtains drawn back give a clue to empty houses. So, if you go out for the evening, close the curtains and put on a light in a front room and, preferably, also at the back of the house which is equally vulnerable. Whether it is day or night when you go out, secure all windows and external doors.

The 'don'ts' include the most glaring one of leaving the door-key under a mat outside or hanging on a string inside the letter box, fitting only a simple latch on the inside of the front door and having a letter-flap through which a thief can put his hand and open the door and leaving a bathroom window open – these windows are generally close to drainpipes which can be easily climbed.

Where there is a flat roof, extra care is needed about window security. Some people leave a small upper window open, especially in an upstairs room, but this is not advised as it can still be sufficiently large to allow someone to open it to its full extent and clamber in, or can provide access when trying to reach the handle of a casement window nearby.

Never keep large amounts of cash in the house. It is far safer to pay bills by cheque or giro, through bank or post office. Never leave a cheque book or savings-bank book lying around the house, and keep credit or bank cards in a different place from the cheque book. Why show a thief what your signature looks like, so that he can sign your cheques with a flourish?

Confidence Tricksters

Most people at some time have encountered the man who knocks on the door and offers to do some work on their home. One of the favourite gambits is to say that there is something wrong with the roof. Years ago we fell for the story that the ridge tiles were slipping at one corner. We gave the so-called builder the money to do the job and a few minutes later he had gone – there was nothing wrong with the tiles and nothing had been done to them. We did not make the same mistake twice.

At the very least you will get a job that is poorly done and over-priced. On the other hand, especially if you are unwise enough to pay in advance or give money for materials said to be needed, you will probably never see your caller again.

Reputable antique dealers do not do door-to-door business. If you want to sell any items, have them properly valued and then make up your mind.

Remember that gas-and electricity meter readers and water-authority representatives all carry identity cards. Ask to see them, unless you recognise your caller from a previous visit. If still in doubt, shut the door and check by phone that there is a representative working in your area.

Be wary, too, of the girl who rings up to say that her firm would like to use your home as a base for a double-glazing demonstration. People have signed forms agreeing to expensive work because they have not read them carefully or properly understood them.

It is worth remembering that not all crooks look like Fagin or Bill Sykes. Up-market ones wear good suits and drive expensive cars. And not all are men – the charming woman who asks to use your telephone, so when it comes to helping others. Be prepared to find all the jealousy, You can counter the first by offering to make the call for her, while leaving her outside, and the second by closing the door and going to fetch her the glass: do not be surprised if she has gone when you re-open the door.

Do not be too ready to impart information. There is no need to be cagey or point-blank rude, but if your neighbours are away and a stranger asks you if they are on holiday, do not tell him so. Your own plans are also your own business, so when you stop for a chat in a shop or pub, do not inform everyone that you are just off for a fortnight in the Canaries. You may not know the people standing around, but there is a good chance that someone will recognise you and know where you live.

Telephone

What about your telephone? If it is an older-style type, you can change the handset to a modern push-button design and have a plug-in socket. This means that when you go to bed you can take the telephone upstairs with you if there is a second socket fitted in the bedroom. This can be done for a very reasonable fee and has the further advantage that, apart from being able to dial 999 in the event of a break-in, if you are taken ill at any time you can dial for assistance without even having to get out of bed.

With an upstairs-downstairs telephone, it is helpful to write out a duplicate address list, with the telephone numbers of everyone you are likely to need in a crisis, including the doctor and district nurse. If you always keep a torch on a table beside the bed, you will be able to dial at any time, even if a fuse has gone or there is a power cut.

Being able to unplug the telephone has another advantage. If you have to be out of the house for several hours, the sound of a phone ringing for hours on end without being picked up can often be heard by someone just outside the front door. It is a useful guide to a burglar that the house is empty. As nobody can get through to you anyway, it is a good habit to unplug the telephone when going out for the day.

Answering machines have become more popular during recent years, especially with people living alone or working from home. But if someone who is checking on you gets through and picks up your pre-recorded message, you are telling them, in effect, that your home is empty. So before switching on the machine be extra careful about locking up before you leave. It is also possible to record a message which does not make it absolutely clear whether you are in or out, e.g. you can say: 'I'm sorry I can't speak to you at the moment, but I will call you back later' rather than 'Miss X is out. Would you please leave a message'. You can tip off your friends and business contacts about the formula you are using, so that no one will take offence.

'Heavy breathers' can be a nuisance to a woman living alone or whose husband is out a great deal. Having dialled at random and got hold of a woman's voice, they can dial again at any time if they have memorised the number. There are two ways of coping with this. Some people call out to a mythical man in another room, adding an injunction to 'keep those damned dogs quiet'. That way they have given two reasons why the caller might think twice before trying again. Another idea is to buy a cheap whistle and blow on it, into the mouthpiece, as hard as you can. The impact is quite something in the pest's ear.

If you take part in voluntary work, such as a church committee, never let your address and 'phone number appear on any posters which are put up in the porch. If you do, you may have unwelcome callers asking for money, saying that they have been sent by someone else whose name appears on the same list.

When picking up the telephone, always say 'Hello' and do not give your name or number. If asked 'Is Amy Smith there?' just say 'No' not 'No, this is Amy Jones'. Giving the surname, once they have the number, helps the caller to find the address in the local directory. Some callers will ask 'What number is that?' The best reply is 'What number are you calling?', putting the onus on them.

Women sometimes think that if it is a girl's voice at the other end, there is no need for caution. But if someone wants to check out your house, he is just as likely to get a sister or girlfriend to do it as to ring himself.

If you have a limited circle of family and friends, it is worthwhile considering whether or not you need to have your name in the book at all. An ex-directory number does not overcome random nuisance calls, but can certainly save you the annoyance of telephone-selling. If you are listed in the directory, make sure that it is by initials only. The same applies to names on boards at blocks of flats.

Everyone has the right to feel secure in their own homes and to go about the streets in safety. Sometimes that is not easy, but generally it is possible provided they take a few elementary precautions. There is plenty of truth in the old clichés, that a man's home can be his castle and that there is safety in numbers.

SELF DEFENCE

Those coming up to retirement should be able to go into it well equipped to deal with life as it is today, not to accept that muggings, bag-snatching and physical attacks are the norm.

Chief Superintendent Sheila Ward, in charge of women's self defence in the Metropolitan Police, feels strongly about this. As an experienced police officer she is well aware of the problems of ordinary people and the work done to protect them against thugs and bullies.

Women start with the disadvantage that they look on themselves as victims and underestimate their ability to defend themselves. She says: 'Their idea of their vulnerability and their lack of dignity has eroded the quality of their life and their perception of their own worth'.

To counter this problem she worked out a programme for women's self-defence, not for highly-trained young officers but for the average woman up to and beyond pensionable age. A group of women in Lewisham, aged from 55 to 80 years agreed to act as test material for the programme. Before they began the four 2-hour sessions, none of them believed that they had the slightest chance of defending themselves from attack. But at the end, as one put it: 'We do not hug the wall now; we walk in the centre of the pavement and are not afraid'.

Following the trial programme, a number of specially-trained police officers are now instructing women's groups in self-defence, working on the theory that the first principle of defending yourself is not to put yourself in a hazardous situation but, at the same time, recognising that shopping has to be done, people must get to and from work and no one should be confined to their home through fear.

Tied in with this approach is her advice to women to try to break a lifelong habit of treating their handbags as storage for everything they consider valuable. Ninety-nine per cent of women of all ages are guilty of this and it is a reason for their great distress when the bag is stolen.

They may be lucky in not having much cash in it at the time. What upsets them far more is the loss or destruction of everything of sentimental value. Older women, particularly, carry around mementoes – such as the last holiday snap of their late husband or the first letters that their grandchildren wrote to them – and they suffer more than anyone when these are lost or deliberately destroyed.

So she advises: 'Check first with the police and make sure that your home is safe. Then take out only as much money as you need, and nothing which you would grieve over if your bag was stolen'. She also offers two very practical tips to older shoppers. First: 'Try to avoid having a carrier bag in each hand. This limits your ability to defend yourself.' Wheeled baskets are not the perfect shopping solution, but at least they leave one hand free. Her second point: 'Never wind a scarf round your neck and tie the ends at the back. It may look smart from the front, but it is a ready-made garotte for someone who tries to throttle you from the rear'.

Take A Tip

Where better to go for advice to men and women on defending themselves than to a man who instructs a number of élite military units, including British and American Special Forces, Commandos and Paratroops, as well as European security police? James Shortt, an international military advisor specialising in close-quarter battle does all that, as well as teaching self-defence to girls and women.

As he explains, self-defence is nothing to do with taking chances or looking for trouble. Nor is it to do with what he describes as 'a catalogue of sport tricks as found in a number of self-styled self-defence schools'. What it has to do with is awareness – the ability to identify a threat in your environment and avoid becoming a target, to escape from attack and evade pursuit and to follow the rules of 'bash 'n' dash', by meeting an attack and disengaging yourself from it rather than getting into a fight with someone tougher than yourself.

Bad news for those who have always fancied themselves lashing out with a kick to the jaw and a blood-chilling yell. Judo, Aikido and Karate do not come into it. These are leisure-oriented and concentrate on the pursuit of technical excellence. What is needed is the ability to defend yourself if attacked and the confidence that comes from a belief in that ability.

What about physical fitness, especially as you get older? You can still defend yourself, anyway, but if you improve your fitness you will have the bonus of feeling and looking better. Any exercise which improves the breathing, such as yoga or swimming, is recommended as well as exercises which involve movements of the head and strengthening the upper part of the body. To make the hands strong and supple, especially if there is a tendency to rheumatism, take a couple of walnuts in their shells and move them round and round in the palm of your hand.

Many cases of purse-snatching or bag-snatching could be prevented by a few simple precautions. If having a meal outside, never put your bag on the chair next to you, especially with the top open and the purse or wallet visible inside. If you put the bag on the floor under a restaurant table. clamp it between your feet so that there is no risk of walking away and forgetting it. Never leave a purse on top of a supermarket basket or trolley. It is better to let the cashier fume while you search for it at the bottom of your bag than have it snatched away at the check-out. Seven purses were taken in 1 hour at our local supermarket due to women forgetting this rule.

Keys should never be kept in a handbag together with your address. It is expensive to have locks changed, but that is what you will have to do if your keys are stolen and the thief knows where you live. Men are better provided with pockets, whether casually or formally dressed, but although women's coats and rainwear have them, many jackets do not, and there are not always pockets in a skirt or dress. However, it is possible to buy ready-made pockets big enough to take keys and to zip them into a side seam.

In his book *Self-Defence – an Essential Handbook* - and it is all of that – James Shortt points out: 'A growing form of car crime is one where car owners are robbed while stopping at traffic lights. Women are particularly susceptible because they often place their handbags on the front passenger seat while driving. The thief then simply opens the unlocked front passenger door and takes the bag, leaving the owner sitting there quite helpless to react'. The answer, he says, is to lock all the car doors when driving.

Another car crime which is avoidable applies to both men and women. A woman will drive to a park to take the dog for a walk. She does not want to be lumbered with a handbag, so just takes the car keys, leaving the bag under the seat. Sometimes a man will do the same thing, leaving his briefcase on the back seat. Neither of them will notice the person sitting in a parked car a little way away and are very surprised on their return to find a window broken and their belongings gone. A car alarm will help, but it pays to be extra careful and to take anything important with you, or to lock it in the boot.

Two of the most unsafe places for most people are banks and post offices. If you have to draw out money or collect a pension, it is best to team up with a friend so that you can keep an eye on each other. Even better, arrange for the pension to be paid directly into your bank and draw out only what you need from time to time. Above all, do not stroll out of the bank or post office stuffing notes into your bag, or pause at the entrance to count them. Again, as a general rule, carry no more money than you can afford to lose.

Some people like to pay bills personally in cash and get a receipt.But if you read the wording on invoices such as those for gas, water or electricity you will find that, even if you are sending a cheque by post, you can get a receipt if you indicate that you want one. It is all in the small print, although you may need a magnifying glass to see it. It is worth a second-class stamp to pay by post rather than risk walking around with anything between £50 to £200 in your bag or wallet. So, wherever possible, use giro or cheques more and cash less.

When it is necessary to go out after dusk, try to keep to busy streets which are well lit. Avoid taking short cuts over waste ground and, if you go for a regular jog or to exercise the dog, vary your route rather than follow exactly the same one night after night.

Ex-SAS man Paul Rice warns: 'Don't walk near the edge of the pavement or you may have your handbag snatched by a motor-cycle pillion passenger or worse, you may be dragged into a car.' Walk facing the traffic, while at the same time keeping an eye open for clumps of bushes or darkened doorways opening on to the pavement.

For general protection, the shrill portable type of alarm is a practical idea. These can be carried in a pocket or bag and let off a sufficiently loud noise to attract attention to the would-be thief. They are an effective deterrent at a low cost.

9 OPPORTUNITIES FOR WORK

It may be that you have not yet come up to pensionable age and still have commitments such as the remainder of a mortgage to pay off, or a teenage family still costing you money even if they are receiving grants for further education.

In that case, a job will be a necessity and, the nearer you get to 60/65, the less likely will be the prospects. But the picture is still far from gloomy.

BEFORE YOU RETIRE

Assuming that you have budgeted realistically for your basic necessities, you can work out how much you need to earn to bring your income up to its present level. Then, before retiring from your present employment, start off by letting as many people as possible know that you propose to continue working after you have officially retired. A year before you stop working at your present job is a good date to begin this. It takes time for the word to get around after you have told your bank manager, business acquaintances or members of clubs to which you belong. Time is important; you are always more likely to get fixed up with something you want if you do not appear to be in a desperate hurry. You also carry more weight when the people you contact know that you are in employment and are able to decide whether the job offered is worth your while.

At the same time it is necessary to be realistic. No one is going to put all the responsibility of a company on someone who may perhaps decide in a few years that he would be happier pottering about at home. So inevitably jobs taken on around the 60s tend to be at a rather lower level.

It is different for those with multiple company directorships, or for top-level judges, who it seems can totter on for years without showing any effects of ageing!

It is quite common to pick up a job through the grapevine, if it is known that you will be doing something when you retire. The scope is quite large, although there will be more part-time than full-time work. That is all to the good, because you will have the extra money and the interest from still working, yet not be too tired to enjoy the company of your wife and to go out together more – often at less cost and with fewer crowds because you can do so at non-peak times.

FINDING A JOB

One of the best guides seen for a long time is Judith Humphries' *Part-Time Work*. This covers a very wide range of employment and shows how it is possible to continue with a professional career, whether it is in law, medicine, veterinary work, teaching, translating, indexing or editorial work. Equally, it tackles the more routine and less demanding jobs, and gives good advice on job-sharing and homeworking, together with plenty of information on employee rights and benefits and the latest job legislation.

There are specialist agencies, such as Success After Sixty or Part-Time Careers, which offer a service that you are not going to get from the standard-type agency or from Job Centres, which are naturally geared more towards younger people.

Success After Sixty offers plenty of employment through its central London office and also has branches in Croydon, Manchester, Slough and Watford. It caters mainly for office work of various grades.

Part-Time Careers specialises, as its name indicates, in careers for people who wish to work part-time. The greatest choice goes to the most flexible – able to work by the day, in the morning or afternoon, and in either half of the week. The emphasis is on secretaries for top executives, although work is also available for graduates with specialist skills. They meet the needs of employers who would rather pay well for a tip-top part-timer than have a mediocre full-timer. However, if you want to get into these openings, it is essential to bring your skills up to date if they have become rusty. Modern offices can be very sophisticated centres of electronic aids and are a far cry from those of 20 years ago with their manual typewriters and simple switchboards.

At times of unemployment, an older person may be inclined to query whether he should take a part-time job that might be available to a younger person. In practice, this does not crop up as much as one might think. It is very seldom that a job designed for one will suit the other, particularly if it is part-time, which it is likely to be. A young man or woman generally needs to earn full-time. The older person, at or approaching pensionable age, is better advised to go for a shorter working week, whether it takes the form of mornings or afternoons, or certain specified days. This applies even more to a married woman. Running a home can be a tiring job and there is no point in continuing to do two jobs (home and outside) every day, unless it is absolutely necessary.

Some firms taper off employees' working arrangements in the year or so before retirement, reducing a 5-day week to 4, 3 or 2 days. This is feasible in some cases and many employees would like to have the opportunity to do it but, from the employers' point of view, there are obvious drawbacks. It can only really be applied to a job which does not have to dovetail with the work of other people in the firm, and it does not suit an employer if someone with a supervisory job is only there for part of the time. Someone else will have to take control when he or she is not around and there is no guarantee that the decisions made will be the same as the absent person's would have been. From the employee's point of view, too, part-timers could well find themselves at the end of the telephone on their 'free' days, with the boss or with their own deputy sorting out problems. So they could end up feeling resentful that, being paid now for 2 days, they are in fact still working for 5.

The advice generally given to retired people is not to reply to advertisements or to put in 'work wanted' advertisements. This makes sense as age is always asked for and it can mean that you do not get short-listed for a job, however good your qualifications. There are various reasons for this. The company's pension scheme is probably not designed to be top-heavy with people over 40. The executive putting in the advertisement may be almost half your age and convinced that everyone near his Dad's age is geriatric. There may be genuine opportunities for promotion in the firm and a young person who grows up with the company may be what they are seeking. The effect of a stream of rejections is to sap your confidence, so advertised jobs are best left alone, unless they make it clear that there is really no upper age limit. Putting in your own advertisements generally is a time-waster. People we know who have done it have not received any replies. Others who have had answers have found themselves a target for a great deal of mail-order literature – but no jobs, plenty of offers of loans, and no shortage of wonderful opportunities for commission-only selling!

ADVISORY SERVICES

What government services are there? First of all, there is the Empoyment Service Division of the Manpower Services Commission, which is responsible for all local employment offices and Job Centres, and also for the Occupational Guidance Service. These bodies deal with manual jobs and with secretarial and clerical appointments. Technical, professional and managerial work is dealt with by the Professional and Executive Recruitment (PER) Service – free to applicants but with a charge for employers. The PER runs free courses to help you get the sort of job you want. Alternatively you can go on a free training or refresher course run by the Training Services Division (TSD) which runs the Training Opportunities Scheme. This can be very useful if you have been out of your own line for some time and want to get back into it but need to update your skills. Naturally the emphasis is on younger people, but those at or approaching retirement have also found these schemes an advantage. It is best to check first with the training officer at the local Job Centre.

The Institute of Directors runs its own retirement advisory bureau and helps members regarding employment after they have retired. This may be a full-time job at home or abroad in the case of an ex-director in his 50s, but much of the work available will be part-time, such as a consultancy on a one-off or on-going basis.

You can also try the Citizens' Advice Bureau (CAB) or the local office of the Social Services Department. The CAB and the DHSS are generally extremely helpful and there is sometimes part-time work available on their own staffs.

PART-TIME WORK

There are certain jobs where a full-time employee would not be needed, but the work-load of full-timers is too much to allow them to take on the extra duties. There are other instances where sickness or holiday relief jobs are available and others where the hours and days worked rule out having someone full-time.

Such jobs include: curator of a small local museum with very limited opening hours; relief at the local branch of a public library during staff holidays; preparing VAT returns for local shops which do not go to an accountant for this work; interviewing for market research firms; distributing give-away magazines or newspapers – sometimes at railway stations, sometimes from door to door; part-time teaching at an adult training centre, using your specialised knowledge and experience; acting as treasurer to one of the smaller charities which has little or no full-time staff. Reliefs are also needed as doctors' and dentists' receptionists, telephonists, typists and cashiers or assistants in local shops.

There are work centres run by the Employment Fellowship. Here the work is very simple – direct mail, packing, sorting, but it provides companionship and you get paid for it.

For someone with the energy, and without commitments, it is possible to take more than one part-time job, such as one requiring 2 days a week and another involving weekend work. But a word of warning: do not overdo it. There is no point in running yourself into the ground if you do not have to. You have worked hard for years and, even if you are a workaholic, you still need some leisure. Work in retirement should provide an interest, the companionship of working with colleagues – unless you prefer to go it alone – and the contrast we all need between work and recreation. Too much work is as destructive as too much leisure. For a married couple this is even more essential. You do not want, later on, to regret that you missed having a few years' leisure together before you were too tired or ill to enjoy it.

SELF-CREATED JOBS

On three occasions, in our own experience, a hobby has led to paid-for work. One was photography, which changed from amateur to professional, as pictures were needed to accompany articles written for magazines. The second was model-engineering, which led to features on the subject, editing of a specialist journal and, later, to opening a model shop. The third one was do-it-yourself, which later formed the basis of a book based on practical experience.

One friend 'sold' local shops on the idea of better displays. Having had West End experience, and a flair for display, he uprated the windows of several local shops and, after a while, extended this to arranging plants and flowers for hotels and offices in his area. Another, less artistic but very practical, earned himself a nice little income just by watering the window-boxes and other floral displays of shops and hotels in one corner of the West End. It meant early rising, but that did not worry him because he was used to getting up early in connection with his former work.

Anyone who has tried to get anything mended knows how difficult it is. One of the first signs of a recession is the increase in cards in the newsagents offering all types of repairs. When things become easier, then the difficulties occur again, but there is always scope for someone who is handy – particularly if he has electrical knowledge – and who is also reliable, to top up his pension.

These are just some examples of a make-your-own-job approach. There are literally hundreds of others, and they have the advantage that you can take on as much or as little work as you want.

Garden maintenance is a job that often appeals to someone who is a keen gardener but has spent most of his working life behind a desk. The attraction is that you work at your own pace, on your own, and are able to do so in the open air. It does not suit those who want companionship all the time they are at work, but seems to have a particular appeal to men – and women – who have had too many people and too much pressure to deal with in their working life.

For those who enjoy working with animals, there are receptionists' posts with veterinary surgeons or, if you prefer to go it alone, you can run your own dog-walking agency or even a clipping service.

Having stepped off the treadmill, you do not want to jump on it again, so beware of many of the offers of 'home work' you see advertised. Especially beware of those which want you to invest any money, even if it is only a few pounds. That is the last you are likely to see of it. Rates of pay are very low and payment is often unnecessarily delayed.

Franchising, even in its best form, is not something for the retired. It involves very hard work and you are likely to end up having to put in far more hours than you did in your employed days. Nor is it a practical idea to open a small shop, for the same reason, unless you choose your retail outlet very carefully. Sub-post-offices can be a real headache and newsagents have to get up at unearthly hours and are expected to open however bad they may be feeling, winter or summer. A pub is one of the biggest snares of all. Almost every journalist we know has either yearned to go to some tropical island and write a best-seller, or to open a country pub. Only one we know actually opened a pub and, within a year he and his wife could not rush back to London quickly enough, to recover from a 12 months' saga of long hours, tiring physical work and the never-ending preparation of food and the smell of beer. As he said: 'It almost made me turn teetotal'.

Sometimes there is the chance of a newly-created job in your own company – a function which the management has been considering, but did not yet feel justified in providing because it did not need someone full time. If you know of such a need, then while still in employment, you could sell the idea to them and offer yourself for the post.

One woman clerical worker who was also a very good cook, had noticed that arrangements for entertaining customers were not particularly good – the canteen was not suitable and the nearest restaurant was so-so and always crowded. Before her retirement date came up, she discussed this with the General Manager and offered to provide a well-cooked well-served meal in one of the directors' offices, when VIP customers were visiting the factory. He was a little doubtful to begin with, but the first effort was such a success that she was retained, on a self-employed basis, to cater for all these functions. By agreement with the company she was allowed to offer a similar service to two non-competitive firms in the area.

What she had done, as so many self-employed people do, was to set her own date for actual retirement at some time in the future to suit herself. She was in complete control of how much work she was prepared to do and she was turning an enjoyable hobby into a profitable business.

A man who had noticed that none of the offices in his area were large enough to have a staff canteen, built up a sandwich-delivery service which was cheap to run and which grew rapidly. Much of the work could be done overnight, using a small fridge, and he soon acquired a good reputation because the sandwiches were excellent value, spotlessly packaged and always arrived on time.

Two women friends opted to start a vineyard. They bought some 4 acres in Sussex and planted vines on half of it after the land had been drained. This produced enough for nearly 5,000 bottles at the first crop, and almost doubled that amount the following year. The grapes are sent away to be made into wine which sells both locally and in London. As yet the vineyard is not making much money, but it is an enjoyable occupation and a very pleasant way to spend retirement.

There are innumerable ways in which to add to your pension or to make a new career for yourself. Some will only bring in a few pounds, but others can absorb all your energy and grow into sizable businesses.

Do you enjoy working with children? There are opportunities during term-time for 'dinner ladies' or assistants at play-groups for under 5s. If there is no play-group in your locality, why not start one, either on your own or with a friend? Crossing wardens are also needed for schools on busy roads and a part-time caretaker of pensionable age could be the solution for schools where a full-time worker is not justified.

Are you interested in antiques? A hairdresser with this hobby became so involved with this that, at 40, she sold her hairdressing salon and spent her time buying and selling antiques from her home. Another woman of the same age, working 4 days a week, spent the fifth day working up a second occupation by taking a bric-a-brac stall at the local covered market.

Are you a good handyman and artistic too? Many do-it-yourselfers are, as their homes bear witness. Dolls' houses and their miniature furniture cost very high prices nowadays. It is possible to buy kits and add individual touches of your own, or to build from scratch, making not only homes of many periods but also the old-time shops which have recently become a vogue.

Are you a good after-dinner speaker? It is well worth working up your material to form the basis of interesting and entertaining lectures. If you own a camera, you can produce slides to illustrate these. There are agencies which provide speakers and, if you have specialist knowledge and an attractive way of presenting it, they will be interested.

We have touched on just a few of the self-created jobs which people have started but a large number of others spring to mind – from carrying out hairdressing in clients' own homes to doing market surveys for firms, either at the street corner or door to door. One real need is for someone reliable to wait in for workmen who have promised to carry out repairs for someone who is at work all day, to keep them well supplied with tea, and to telephone the owner about progress or any problems that have arisen. This is a service which is vital in an area where everyone in the street is out at work and there are no good neighbours with whom keys can be left.

Some outlets which appear to be likely are best given a wide berth. Hot-dog stands, ice-cream vans and window-cleaning all seem to be good openings, but in some areas these are very strictly shared out between the existing operators and someone who tries to muscle in may regret it. So, ask around and get some idea of the form before you invest in a ladder or a truck.

LOOKING AFTER HOMES

An insistence that all applicants must be *over* 40 is such a rarity these days that people immediately sit up and take notice. Even more so when they learn that 40 is only the start and that there is no upper age limit.

This is a requirement of Homesitters, a specialist agency started by advertising man Michael Shepherd-Smith and his wife a few years ago. This supplies people going away on holiday or business with someone who will stay in their home, look after their pets, and generally keep an eye on things until they return. Vetting of the homesitters needs to be very strict and the agency requires references from two professional people (e.g. bank manager, lawyer) who have known the applicant for at least 5 years, plus two character references, as well as recent employment references. In fact, as they say, they must know what the applicant has been doing for the last 20 years.

Once that hurdle is over, Homesitters try to match the client who wants a sitter with the sitters available, taking into account the preferences of each. This seems to work very well and, in many cases a friendship develops, and the family will ask for the same sitter whenever they go away.

Pets are a very important consideration. Canda Sherwell of Homesitters says: 'I think we have had homes with every breed of dog, over the last few years. One housed fourteen St Bernards'. Sometimes a family has had to go away at the time when their bitch was whelping and a calm, knowledgeable sitter has been a godsend. Other pets have included donkeys, ponies, a wide range of small furry mammals and she-goats – where a knowledge of how to milk a goat has been a great asset on the part of the homesitter. Some animals are more exotic – one house contained free-flying humming birds and another had a fire-belly toad whose diet of live crickets had to be specially obtained.

Home sitting appeals to many people in the 55-65 age bracket and there are always more applicants than jobs. The ideal sitter is someone who is free of commitments, who likes seeing various parts of the country and staying in different types of home. They must be prepared to undertake 'sits' for 12 weeks in a year. They receive modest pay, travelling expenses each way and accommodation and board are provided. The client provides for one person, but the sitter is allowed to bring a companion who has to be responsible for his/her food, so the work is well suited to a retired man and wife.

The 'sit' usually covers a house, garden and pets, but on occasions there may be an elderly relative who is fit, and not in need of any nursing, who will remain in the house during the family's absence. In that case, sitter and client can come to a private arrangement about looking after the old lady or gentleman, sharing meals with them and helping to keep them amused.

WORKERS' CO-OPERATIVES

There is another approach to working for yourself which has become more popular recently. This is the workers' co-operative. In some cases, workers faced with redundancy have continued an existing business on a co-operative basis, taking it over from the present owners. In others, they have started fresh businesses from scratch. Some local authorities will give useful advice on this point, In the Croydon area, the

Co-operative Development Agency of the Croydon Community Relations have organised free courses for people interested in starting up such a venture.

SMALL BUSINESSES

A number of successful individual businesses have been started with a golden handshake from a firm which has had to make people redundant because the company has been taken over or has merged with another, so that many jobs are then being duplicated. The same applies as to businesses started with a gratuity after World War 2. The difference is that there is now far more help for small businesses, both in the form of advice and of grants, which did not exist then.

All the same, the failure rate among small businesses continues to be high. High-interest rates have played their part but there are other reasons: going into a field which is already overcrowded; knowing nothing about the line you have decided to open in; unwillingness to change your lifestyle to suit a growing business. It pays to ask for advice from people with experiences of small businesses: first of all, the Small Firms Information Centres. They can offer a free 2-week course plus useful free booklets covering every aspect of running your own business. Details are available through your local Professional Executive Recruitment (PER) office, or the head office at 4 Grosvenor Place, London SW1.

It is not necessary to take all the advice you are given – you would probably never get started if you did, as bank managers tend to be less than optimistic and often accountants look towards minimising tax as a first consideration. You have got to make up your own mind after hearing their views. There is nothing wrong with relying on a hunch because it is going to be your business and your hunches are the only ones to follow.

If setting up in business you will certainly need the services of an accountant. He will reduce your tax to a minimum and let you know the many expenses you can claim of which you may not be aware. Also, his caution will prevent you being talked into too early an expansion, which often takes place when the first large contract is secured.

10 VOLUNTARY WORK

We hope that you may now have fixed up a part-time job or started a business of your own which does not take up every day of the week. You will then have some time to spare for leisure and for helping others. If you are fortunate enough not to need to supplement your pension, you will have even more opportunity to play a part in the community. For many people retirement is the first chance they have had of giving their services. For others, who already did some voluntary work in their spare time, it is now possible to do a bit more.

Retired people have plenty to offer. They always have, but now that early retirement is on the increase, there are men and women who can contribute a good deal more. They can offer experience, organising ability and a recent background in industry, commerce or one of the professions, as well as the energy and enthusiasm of someone still at their peak.

Taking it from the top, the British Executive Service Overseas, started in conjunction with the Institute of Directors, arranges for volunteers to work in developing countries. The appointments are unpaid, but travelling and living expenses are met and those who take up this work must be prepared to go for a quite a long time to very remote places. This work can be undertaken by either single or married people.

At the simplest level, helping may mean calling in for a chat with someone who is housebound and lives alone. Changing library books, taking an elderly person to church in your car, posting letters for them or, if necessary going further and writing these letters, all take up very little time but are terrific morale-boosters for the recipient.

Listening is probably the greatest single help which anyone can give.

Irrespective of age, sex or general circumstances, we all need someone to listen to us from time to time. So if this is your form of helping, follow the rules of good listening: never yawn or glance at your watch; do not try to hurry the narrative along by finishing someone else's story – you are bound to get it wrong; when you leave, thank them for an interesting talk – even if the ratio of conversation was actually 90 per cent to them and only 10 per cent to you.

If you decide to do something for your neighbours, do not make the mistake of taking on too much. Small things loom large to people on their own all day and they come to look forward to them. It is much better to look after two neighbours in this way and always be reliable about dates and times than to try to take on the whole street and only be able to keep one promise in ten.

ORGANISATIONS CONCERNED WITH VOLUNTARY WORK

Before committing yourself to any form of voluntary work, we suggest you find out more about the whole field which is open to you.

Where can you go to find out? As usual, the public library is one of the first places to visit. Most reference departments have a copy of the *Charities Digest*, an annual publication of the Family Welfare Association, or the *Voluntary Social Services Directory and Handbook* of the National Council of Social Service. Study them to see if there is one particular form of service which appeals to you. The London Council of Social Services publishes a booklet *Someone Like You Can Help*, which is a guide to several hundred national voluntary organisations and how they can use your time and skills. It is also well worth contacting a branch of the Pre-Retirement Association, to find out how you can help in increasing membership as well as participating in voluntary work already being carried out by branch members.

The next place is the Citizens' Advice Bureau, whose staff call on professional services of all kinds; if they cannot answer a question, it is highly likely that no one else can.

The WRVS (Women's Royal Voluntary Service) operates throughout the UK and provides meals-on-wheels, clubs, homes for the elderly, chauffeuring to and from hospitals and manning of trolley shops in hospitals, apart from always being on the scene when there is a disaster and emergency help is needed. It is not only for women – men have been among the volunteers ever since it started.

Thirty per cent of retired people live alone and that figure will increase. Most prefer to continue to live in their own homes, but they need help to do so safely and happily. Help the Aged is an organisation which sets out to assist by providing funds for schemes which allow them to stay on in their own homes and, at the same time, for the extra care and support needed by those who have become too frail to manage alone and who now live in sheltered housing.

The help includes minibuses to transport disabled old people to clubs, and centres where elderly victims of a stroke can re-learn daily living skills and where pensioners may be able to find congenial companionship. Their education department does a great job in supplying a wide range of teaching and training materials for schools, to increase awareness of the needs of the elderly. Very important – it also shows ways in which older people can help the younger generations and their Side-By-Side scheme concentrates on ways of bringing the young and old together.

A typical project, carried out at Newcastle-upon-Tyne and co-funded with the organisation Shelter, concentrated on technical help over repairs, dealing with finance, grants where applicable, liaising with building societies, getting estimates for work and carrying out independent checks on the completion of the work. This is one of a number of projects organised on a co-operative basis with other charitable organisations.

The monthly newspaper *Yours* is a valuable source of information on all matters affecting older people.

Another organisation, which has the self-explanatory title of 'Age Concern', does a great deal on behalf of the elderly, organising holidays, providing transport, running luncheon clubs and training volunteers in the care of old people. This started off in 1940 as the National Old People's Welfare Council. Today there are national organisations in each of the other three countries within the UK – Scotland, Wales and Northern Ireland – independent but working closely with Age Concern (England) and with each other. This organisation sets out to improve the standard and quality of life of older people, maintains close contacts with MPs of all parties, operates an information department that keeps up with the frequent changes of legislation and government policy and runs a research unit that produces a series of reports on aspects of life for the elderly. It has also commissioned its own surveys, which have had considerable impact on social policy.

Age Concern run courses, seminars and conferences for professionals and volunteers working with elderly people, as well as giving cash aid to local organisations, which develop new services, or to self-help groups of pensioners. Booklets such as *Your Rights* are simple, comprehensive guides to all the benefits which are available to retired people and *Your*

Taxes and Savings offers useful information on financial matters for the retired. At local level, groups offer a whole range of services in their area: good neighbour schemes, holidays, transport to lunch clubs and day centres, practical help by volunteers in decorating homes or tending gardens, visiting housebound and disabled, and meals on wheels. More recently a hospital after-care scheme has been started, helping elderly people cope with the transition from hospital to home. Here are just a few of the services which have been pioneered and are now well established: training of staff in residential homes, counselling services, crime prevention, family support and services for those elderly who are mentally infirm, employment bureaux and chiropody.

Both Help the Aged and Age Concern have the same common aim of improving the quality of life for the elderly, so both organisations often work together on a number of matters. They also work with the Centre for Policy on Ageing, which provides research and information for professionals and policy-makers. While Age Concern is mainly occupied with providing services through local groups in the UK, Help the Aged is chiefly active in fund-raising for projects in the UK and around the world. Outside the UK, it supports self-help projects for the elderly in the Third World, as well as emergency relief and medical aid.

Addresses of all these organisations can be found in the local telephone directories. If you experience any difficulty over this, the public library or the nearest branch of the Citizens' Advice Bureau will be able to assist.

CHOOSING A VOLUNTARY ACTIVITY

You might prefer to do voluntary work for people of a different age group, or for animals. You might feel strongly about plans for a new motorway, about preserving the environment, or you might be a committed supporter of one of the political parties. You might even enjoy the prospect of flexing your mental muscles in support of a whole variety of causes.

One of the bonuses of doing voluntary work is that it brings you in contact with people of a very wide range of ages, from schoolchildren to the over-80s and, in many areas, with people of different classes, creeds and colours. There is nothing like a keen feeling for justice or of righteous anger to unite people. In those circumstances, everything else is forgotten and people speak with one voice.

If you are a person who must go into everything 100 per cent, that is fine. You will do it whatever advice you are given and, no doubt, will do a lot of good and get a lot of satisfaction out of it. But most people like to be able to do something but not to dedicate the rest of their life to it. However many hours you can spare, remember that you should give a professional standard even though you are a volunteer. If you are giving your services, then they should be your best. That is the idea behind the advice given to retired people to proceed cautiously – 1 hour of professional help is worth a whole day of amateur bumbling.

Sit down and have a think about the type of service you are prepared to offer. If you know you cannot stand the sights, sounds and smells of poverty, face the fact and do not volunteer for the kind of work which involves these. If you feel awkward with people who are senile, you will not make a good job of helping them and, if illness frightens you, then you are unlikely to give much support to those who are seriously ill. But – you may be a wizard at interpreting bureaucratic jargon and filling in answers for people who get scared stiff at the sight of a printed form. You may be an extremely efficient home-decorator, or electronics could be child's play to you. In your working life you would not have dreamt of applying for jobs for which you had no aptitude, so why volunteer for them in your private life as a retired person?

On the other hand, quite often someone retired is looking for a complete change from their working life. A man used to having responsibility for a staff of thousands might prefer to do a simple manual job, while another – especially if it is an early retirement – might want to keep his organising abilities in trim. It pays to spend an evening jotting down what you really enjoy doing: working with a team, or on your own; dealing with people or with computers, documents, accounts or committees; coping with all types of individuals from the well-meaning to the downright cussed; dealing with the young rather than with your own age group; or working to give animals a better deal while keeping human contacts to the minimum.

If you are a lawyer, bank manager or accountant, you will probably have to fend off people who want you to become chairman of a committee, treasurer or appeals organiser. This is fine if you want to do it and are well equipped but not so good, though, if your first impulse on retiring is to get as far away as possible from the work of a lifetime. So stand firm and insist on helping in your own way. It may be that you will be more useful as a loner than as a joiner.

In joining any group activity, do not expect your fellow workers to be saints. They are only human but at least they are trying to be a bit more so when it comes to helping others. Be prepared to find all the jealousy, backbiting and even obstruction that you thought you had left behind in the business world. There are as many people on ego trips in voluntary set-ups as among those clawing their way to the top in management or the higher echelons of trade unionism.

A well-known Jesuit once said: 'Most of our crosses come walking towards us on two legs'. If you do voluntary work, you will have to be prepared to tolerate people, just as you had to put up with them at work, unless you want to develop ulcers through sheer irritation.

Do not be a martyr, taking on too much and becoming exploited. If you are a compulsive martyr, try to keep it in the home and avoid disorganising any useful activity outside by shouldering everyone else's burdens and then collapsing under them, leaving a nice state of chaos to be sorted out by someone else.

Another 'don't': if you have a partner at home, still allow time for him or her in your busy life. A wife can be a charity widow just as much as a golf widow and could end up seeing less of you than she did when you were employed. So be content to lend a hand from time to time – after all, you are supposed to be taking things more easily now.

OTHER ACTIVITIES

Voluntary work does not necessarily require a charitable basis to be useful. There are any number of organisations – youth clubs, ecology groups, cycling clubs, allotment societies – which need someone to do a bit of routine paperwork and keep members in touch with what is going on. There is a whole range of other bodies where people with skills and experience can be useful such as the Red Cross, St John Ambulance and Rotary Clubs, football or basketball clubs may require coaches or referees and the local hospital's League of Friends often needs help with the telephone trolley in the wards, staff for out-patients' canteens, or script-writers for hospital radio.

But the biggest appeal to most people is activities that help those in greatest need. They may be the very old or the very young and include battered wives, widowers struggling to do the best for their children and still hold down a job, people of any age who have been the victims of street crime or of attacks in their home and convalescent people who miss the back-up of a hospital in the first few weeks on returning home.

There are other ways of helping, to which not everyone is suited. The Samaritans, who do a terrific job in dealing with people of all ages who are acutely depressed or suicidal, have to screen their helpers to make sure that they have the 'bottle' to take on this very arduous work. Prison-visiting and the caring for prisoners' families also requires a calm and experienced as well as a sympathetic approach.

Do not be surprised if your offer of help is not accepted immediately. There may be someone who is doing exactly what you are prepared to do. Have a second string. If you do not take on too much, you may be able to help with both if the chance occurs later.

If you have kept up your driving licence after retirement, and especially if you have kept your car, your assistance will be particularly welcome by many local organisers, whether it is in collecting jumble, distributing newsletters, or ferrying Scouts and Guides to weekend camps. With the high cost of petrol, rotas need to be worked out and the number of vehicles kept to a minimum. With other driver-helpers you can organise an efficient routine, sorting out shifts so as to keep down mileage and yet provide a good service.

Some of the best forms of voluntary service are help given between individuals – friends or neighbours. Do not think that because you are frail and elderly that you have nothing to contribute. One of the most positive attitudes we have come across was shown by an old lady in a residential home. She found that too much leisure was a drag and, as she was an expert needlewoman, she asked all her visitors to bring her any mending that needed doing. It was a two-way benefit – she stopped herself becoming bored, and when visitors called on her with flowers or fruit from their gardens there was a neat pile of mending ready for them to take away.

Ironing is not a popular task, and even in these days of drip-dry clothes there are still some that need to be pressed. With constant washing or injudicious tumble-drying the creaseless finish stops working, so that a light run-over with the iron is needed. One pensioner we know took on the ironing for two of her younger neighbours, in return for getting her lawn mown. Because she was home all day, she had the ironed clothes waiting when the younger people came home in the evening ready to go out for a meal or disco. Another, who always had a large amount of washing to take to the launderette, picked up the laundry for several of her neighbours who were out at work and did not own washing machines.

Caring For The Sick And Elderly
How many middle-aged people in your area are caring for an elderly relative who needs constant attention, or for an incurably ill husband or wife? It is reckoned that this unstinting care saves the State some 5 billion pounds a year, but the toll it takes of the lives of the people concerned is something that cannot be priced. They have no desire to shirk the task, but unlike nursing staff they have no off-duty hours.

Although neighbours are often ready to help with shopping, they cannot be expected to take over any of the more demanding work.

Apart from finding out what you can do to assist directly – perhaps by sitting with the patient for a couple of hours to allow the carer a rest – you can join with others in lobbying Government for a fairer deal for the families concerned. One of the ways in which some of that 5 billion could be spent is by increasing the number of community nurses, so that there is a greater amount of professional assistance in the patients' homes, not a brief visit from an overworked nurse who finds it difficult to complete her rounds in the time allotted.

Another way to assist is by supporting the hospices' movement which already does a tremendous job in caring for the terminally ill of all ages. There is a growing number of hospices but more are needed. They are able to cater for those for whom at present there is no cure, who require professional nursing in a relaxed and cheerful atmosphere. Visiting hours are as long as family and patient need and, on occasions, have even included the family pet. The hospice is concerned with the whole family, and their need for support and counsel. They are able, which a busy hospital is not, to devote more time to each patient and to encourage relatives to assist in many ways, so that the nursing becomes a shared undertaking from which the patient can derive great benefit.

Another sphere where help is needed is that of impressing on Government the vital necessity of a telephone for elderly people living alone. It is absurd that water, gas and electricity cannot be cut off without contacting the Department of Health and Social Security, but a telephone line can be cut off without any such reference. Yet how can someone in difficulties dial 999 without leaving their home, or summon any other type of help? This is something which should be brought under the same regulations without delay. Failing that, then simple alarm devices should be provided for OAPs, readily accessible and in more than one room.

Campaigning

There may be something, about which you have held strong views, that is happening or about to happen, in your area. When working, you were probably too busy to do more than contribute money towards fund-raising or add your signature to a petition. Now you have more leisure, you can be active in organising petitions, circularising residents or contacting local councillors. It may be a dangerous crossing or junction that needs to be improved, or better lighting provided in a short cut so that more people could use it with safety. Someone who is not keeping typical business hours is able to deal with council offices, most of which are closed by the time that those still working get back home. Someone able to deal with officialdom is invaluable, as usually those at home when officials are around are those least able to take them on (Murphy's Law again).

Public inquiries generate an enormous amount of work and, if you have views on where a proposed motorway, reservoir or leisure centre should be sited, your services will be extremely important, especially if you have an engineering, statistical or planning background.

There are meetings to be held on whether or not to have a barrister to speak for your group and who is to brief him. It may be decided that two or more small groups may share the cost of legal representation. After the decision, there is a great deal of work in writing letters, keeping the media informed (and even more important, keeping them interested) and organising a supply of press cuttings so that you can counter statements by the opposition without delay.

Where an issue cuts across barriers of age, sex or class, you have considerably more helpers to call upon, plus the stimulation of working with people who bring an entirely different viewpoint to the same subject. However old you get you can still learn and some of the best ideas we have been given have come from people a quarter of our age. Do not be put off a cause you believe to be right if some of your fellow workers go about their protests in a way you find unacceptable. Generally a level-headed approach with checked-out facts, presented in an articulate way, is more impressive. But there is usually also room for a more emotional one, which is likely to get more headlines. It may not be your scene, but do not underestimate its value in complementing your own technique.

11 ENJOYING YOUR LEISURE

GARDENING

A walk along any street in the UK quickly reveals the love of growing plants among people of all ages.

One decision to be made on retirement is whether to look for a home with a big garden so as to be able to indulge this interest to the full. It can be very successful, and television programmes have shown a number of huge spaces that have been tamed and beautified by people of retirement age. However, should you opt for the big and beautiful, do not forget that, should circumstances change, you can retrieve the situation and still retain a lovely garden.

The traditional English garden was generally composed of sections that locked into each other. It frequently started with a terrace. Then came lawns and flowerbeds and, finally, a shrubbery. If a kitchen garden was included, this was usually sited at one side of the main plan, with access from the utility areas of the house.

If, in the future, such a garden poses problems, it is possible to extend the lawn so that it covers the original kitchen garden and the flowerbeds, thus reducing maintenance to the regular use of an electric lawnmower and annual lawn-dressing. The kitchen garden could be reduced to a couple of small beds near the back door for herbs and salad vegetables, and the herbaceous borders replaced by a few specimen trees and a variety of conifers. Even the terrace could be planned for minimum maintenance, using shrubs and bulbs in containers. The resulting garden, although covering a large area, involves no more effort in terms of work than one a quarter its size.

Experienced gardeners will know what to do in such a situation. The man who has taken up gardening as a retirement hobby would do best to seek help from a friend and to avoid taking on too big a commitment. Gardeners are generally very willing to pass on information and are often equally generous with cuttings.

At one time it was usual for a retired man to apply for an allotment in order to provide cheap vegetables when his income was reduced. This is less popular now and, in many areas, allotments are being phased out to allow for different use of the land by local authorities. At the same time there has been the development of growing bags that take up very little space in a backyard or small garden. Starting with tomatoes and strawberries, these compost bags are now used for a wide variety of vegetables.

Container-gardening, using a variety of pots, troughs, sinks and barrels, also offers easy-care growing in a small space. Even new potatoes can be grown in a barrel of the type popular for strawberries, and miniature fruit trees will thrive in tubs, using the correct compost and choosing a suitable site.

It must not be forgotten that not all gardens are at ground level. Gardens can be on flat roofs, on balconies, or in basements, and window-boxes can transform the appearance of a house if a bit of imagination is used.

In the case of roof-gardening, the most important considerations are the strength and thickness of the roof and its surface material, and whether or not there are any local bye-laws which would prohibit the use of a roof for this purpose. Having checked on these points, one can go ahead to provide safety by erecting a fence to enclose the garden. This not only prevents people falling over the edge, but gives shade to plants, plus shelter against winds which will be stronger up on the roof than at ground level. Roof gardens may be windy but they also get plenty of sun so that the soil dries out more quickly. It will therefore need very frequent watering and also more fertiliser to replace nutrients washed away.

With the exception of tall and heavy trees, you can grow much the same plants, shrubs and climbers as those found in a garden at ground level. There is, of course, scope to use containers and that means you are not restricted to one type of garden soil. Your plants can range from lime-haters such as rhododendrons, azaleas, and a number of heathers, to those needing an alkaline soil, such as clematis and pinks.

It is always interesting to look down into a well-planned basement garden to see what can be done against the odds. The biggest problem is the lack of light. This can be overcome by painting all wall surfaces white, and by the use of glass to catch and reflect what little sunlight penetrates into the lower-ground-floor area. The floor surface is also highly important and decorative tiling – ceramic, concrete, terrazzo – can form part of a well-designed outdoor room, or what might be called a patio-below-stairs.

There are a surprising range of shrubs and plants that do well in shade, including hypericum, camellias and mahonia, a number of which have decorative foliage, as well as woodland plants and ferns.

Somewhat similar problems apply to balconies as to roofs. The wind is stronger and tends to come in the form of piercing draughts through gaps in the building. The same considerations apply regarding sheltering, watering and the use of fertiliser. There are safety factors to bear in mind when choosing the containers; they should be low set and not likely to fall over the edge of the parapet. It is also necessary, when using cans or a hose for watering, to consider the convenience of those living on the lower floors.

One of the best ways of providing a colourful display, plus variety, is to use plants in individual pots set in a trough containing a sand and peat mix. These can be shunted to the back as they finish flowering and fresh ones brought forward. There is scope for all-year interest, with miniature conifers, heathers, bulbs and colourful climbers, and a sprinkling of hardy annuals.

Your gardening might have to be confined to one or two window-boxes or hanging baskets. Boxes can be made up easily by a do-it-yourselfer, but obviously need to be very securely fixed. To save time, you can pick from a choice of ready-mades in plastic, fibreglass or aluminium. As with balconies and roofs, regular watering – twice daily in summer – is needed, and good regular feeding.

Hanging baskets are another form of mini-gardening that is not fully exploited. Very many plants are suited to this yet one usually only sees half-a-dozen old favourites. The baskets should not have too much – or too little – sun, and need plenty of watering. If it is easy to take down the basket, it can be immersed in water; otherwise if you stand on a chair or pair of steps it can be reached by a watering can.

Some houses are built with so little space that the paving at the rear has to do duty as a garden, a sheltered sitting-out area, and storage space for water-butt and dustbin. Privacy and added shelter can be provided by a range of openwork screens and trellises, used as background to climbers such as clematis and honeysuckle. Some of the ornamental concrete screens can be used as a decorative feature in themselves. Planting can be in narrow beds, or in containers, and tiny plants can be grown between the paving stones. The area is best planted as a whole, with attractive garden furniture making it an extension of the house in warm weather, with the chance to enjoy leisurely outdoor meals now that there is no need to rush back to office or factory.

For all types of gardens, containers offer a great choice of appearance, apart from the facility of using different kinds of soil, already mentioned.

If you want to move them around from time to time, go for lightweights such as plastic or glass fibre. If they are to be kept in a permanent position, the heavier hardwoods, cement or handmade pots can each be used, or different types placed together. Or you may prefer to design your own, or press into service a range of items – old wine barrels, chimney pots, or the stone sinks which you can come across occasionally and which make very delightful trough gardens.

As people get older, it is not so comfortable to spend a long time kneeling, so top of your retirement presents list could be a thick rubber gardening mat, or a pair of the knee pads that serve the same purpose. Another handy device is a seat which converts to a kneeler.

If bending becomes difficult, look for long-handled tools, e.g. hoes, rakes, which can reach easily to the back of the bed without effort. Gardens designed specifically for the disabled include some with a sunken paved centre surrounded by waist-high flower beds, none so deep as to prevent them being reached by a rockery trowel and fork.

To save energy, look out for all the lightweight garden accessories you can, e.g. plastic watering cans make the job much easier than the heavier metal ones.

Always do it the lazy way. If the garden is too small to justify a wheelbarrow, use a bag or box tied on to an old shopping trolley frame for clearing-up jobs such as cutting back perennials or pruning shrubs. If you are stiff when getting up from kneeling, a useful tip is to have a fork well rammed into the soil nearby which you can use as a support.

No garden shed? Then the items constantly used in the garden should be kept in a drawer or cupboard in the house, ready to hand. The traditional gardener's apron, with its full-width pocket, also saves unnecessary trips indoors for secateurs, twine, plant labels and so on.

Spare a thought for your neighbours. If you keep a cat or dog, reserve a space at the end of the garden for a sandpit. If this is provided, a cat will generally use it instead of scratching up your neighbours plants. A dog can be trained to do the same, which reduces problems of pavement fouling.

Although gardening is the hobby most associated with retirement, there is no shortage of others which are equally absorbing.

COLLECTING

Unless you are that rare person who has too much room at home, go for something small. Some of the most attractive antiques shown on that popular television series *The Antiques Roadshow* are quite tiny – thimbles, snuff boxes, Toby jugs and miniatures. If you already have an interest in this direction, now is the time to develop it further. Like so many hobbies, you have the opportunity to look around in your own area or to go further afield in your search. And there is always the chance that if you can bear to part with something you have bought you could also become a dealer in a small way. Advice on market stalls, antique fairs and auction sales where you can pursue your interest can be found in that excellent book *Junk* by David Benedictus.

MODELLING
Modelling Railways

Develop a hobby in which you already have an interest. It might be modelling railways, ships or aeroplanes. For some 14 years, we ran a model shop and the ages of the customers ranged from 9 to 90. Most were male, but as time went on more girls and women began to show a keen interest. This was particularly true of model railways. Even if they had never heard of Gresley or Bulleid, and the names of Maunsell or Stanier meant absolutely nothing to them, they could appreciate the miniature models and the scenic effects. This applied particularly to N gauge, where the whole effect could be achieved in a comparatively small space. This gauge, even more than the larger OO gauge, also had the advantage that, if a move to a smaller house had to be faced, the layout could be more easily accommodated.

Apart from the families who bought only proprietary locomotives and rolling stock, were the dedicated model engineers, who can spend as long as 2 years in scratch-building, and whose workshops are a loco-building works in miniature. Between them and the families who owned a simple layout were the men who assembled white-metal kits and painted and lined them. Like the scratch-builders, they tended to be loners but, with very few exceptions, were always ready to pass on tips to the inexperienced. In fact, the only time that any dissension arose was if there was a passionate dispute between the rival merits of Great Western and the London Midland and Scottish. Even the protagonists of steam versus diesel learned to live together in time.

Whether or not you are interested in building railways, an interesting outing can be had to one of the many preserved lines. Some of the most delightful scenery is to be found in Wales, where there are some seven preserved lines. Of the English counties, Kent has the greatest number, with three of special interest at Tenterden, Romney and Sittingbourne. But whether it is the Highlands of Scotland or the Isle of Man, there are always people who enjoy keeping up the locos and rolling stock and maintaining the track and the signalling system, as well as ensuring that the station is in good condition. Facilities vary from one place to another. In most instances you can ride in the carriages for a relaxed trip of a few miles. At some, refreshments are available, or you can bring your own supplies and have a picnic. Even if you live in London, it is an easy run out to the famous Bluebell Line in Sussex, where some families take a week of their holidays to live on the spot and join in the work of maintenance.

Railway museums also abound and one that is particularly worth a visit is the Railway Museum at York.

Modelling Ships, Cars and Planes

One characteristic of modelling hobbies is that there is an all-year-round interest. One customer, who over the years became a close friend, decided to plan ship-modelling as a retirement hobby. He began by reading through the local library's stock of books on early sailing vessels. Then he visited the Maritime Museum at Greenwich to study drawings and photographs. From the time that he chose ply and balsa, it took 12 months to build his first model ship, but when completed it was well up to the standard of a professional model-maker. Yet his actual job, up to retirement, was nothing to do with ships; he was, in fact, a storeman in a warehouse. He wanted a hobby that would keep his interest whatever the weather. In the summer he spent a lot of time getting about, hunting down materials for his model, not only in model shops but at ships' chandlers, ironmongers etc., to ensure that each component was authentic; in the bad weather he could stay at home and get on with the next stage of construction.

Veteran and vintage cars also have their attraction and here again it is not just the construction of the kit, which might range from the simple to the very complex, but also the range of magazines in which to browse, the number of books available for buying or borrowing, and the visits to car museums such as the well-known Montagu Motor Museum at Beaulieu, as well as the numerous rallies all over the country, particularly the Brighton Run at the beginning of November.

With most aero-modellers, of course, it is the flying which is the main interest. Unlike the builders of locos and sailing ships, the actual construction is a much quicker affair, after which the plane has to be tested and put through its paces outdoors before it can take part in any club event. For many people it is the participation at these events which appeals most, but others go in for it because they are fascinated by the mode of flight – control-line, diesel-engine, radio-control.

Military Modelling
At one time, collectors of model soldiers were thought to be boys playing with toys in the same way as railway modellers were held to be playing with trains. Luckily, that attitude has largely disappeared. It does not take much observation to see the amount of intelligence or knowledge generated by building a complicated railway layout, working out routes and signalling, and fitting it up with locomotives and railway stock. That is one reason why schools are usually very keen to encourage railway-modelling groups. In the same way, any schoolmaster with a history class to handle can see the contribution to be made by the modelling of miniature soldiers.

For many adults – women as well as men – it can be an absorbing hobby. In some cases it may mean looking round for specially-made, ready-painted figures costing quite a sizeable sum, but others can get even more enjoyment from a collection of plastic or metal miniatures, once they have been altered and detailed to fit in with a certain battle scene. A lot of people restrict their choice to a particular period – the Napoleonic is one of the most popular – while others span history from ancient China to D-Day. The best results can be obtained by concentrating on one scale and one period, reading up thoroughly in books and magazines, visiting museums, looking at displays (often put on to raise funds for charity) and watching television programmes.

Not only does the hobby illuminate military history, but a great deal of social history comes into it as well, because civilians, contemporary housing and public buildings are all featured in many diagrams. Two very good books to introduce this subject are *Military Uniforms of the World in Colour* by Prebeu Kannïck and *How to Go Collecting Model Soldiers* by Henry Harris.

Where To Do Your Modelling
This brings us to the point which needs to be settled right at the start – where to do the actual modelling? In theory, the ideal is a spare room – if you have such a thing. But even if you do, many modellers are gregarious people and, after a while on their own, they will trickle back to the living room where the rest of the family are. At the same time, important

components can be accidentally vacuumed away if not cleared up at the end of the day, and there is nothing more calculated to put anyone off a hobby than a long time spent in setting up and putting away rather than actually working at it.

Major Henry Harris puts a good case for the old-fashioned rolltop desk, with its many small drawers, and a lid that comes down and encloses everything when you get up to go to bed, as the ideal answer for the military modeller. This has possibilities also for the loco-builder, but there still remains the matter of the completed layout.

As far as railway-modelling is concerned, at one time or another our layout was housed in turn in almost every room in the house. The bathroom was exempt because it had already been earmarked as a photographic darkroom. The tiny kitchenette worktop saw a vice clamped to it more often than a mincing machine and we needed all four burners on the gas cooker as one was frequently in use for heating the gluepot.

Suitable sites for the actual layout can range from one, two or three sides of a bedroom to an ambitious layout in a loft, or even a foldaway board against a wall. But some of the work can be carried out on smaller sections at one end of the living room, provided these can be covered up satisfactorily until wanted next time. An alternative to a rolltop desk could be one of those ready-made photographic mini-darkrooms, on which the doors can be shut at night and the seat tucked under the worktop, so that no vital bits will get lost.

If there is any objection to this, remind your spouse of the poor woman who was locked out of her bathroom for weeks on end because her husband was testing his model submarine in the bath.

CRAFTWORK FOR THE HOME

Some of the most popular sessions at pre-retirement courses are those dealing with making things for the home. These hobbies can show a worthwhile saving, compared with having the job done professionally. A friend of ours for years had made practically all the family's clothes. As they grew up and left home she found more time on her hands, so enrolled in a soft-furnishings class at the local evening institute. Being already competent at making clothes, it did not take her long to make curtains, bedspreads and chair covers which had a professional look. She then went on to tackle real upholstery so that she was able to deal with the Edwardian and Victorian pieces which she was able to pick up at auctions.

How good are you at crochet? Finding herself with extra leisure at 60, another friend – skilled at both crochet and knitting – decided to get away from making jumpers and started on a crocheted bedspread. A few months later she had an exquisite white spread that would have cost pounds at a luxury store and which is destined to become a family heirloom in the years to come. It was all done while watching television during winter evenings.

Both of us have always admired patchwork. At its simpler level it is one of the easiest handcrafts to master. Bundles of offcuts are obtainable from places such as the Laura Ashley shops in the UK and the templätes can be obtained from craft centres. There are plenty of books on patchwork in libraries, including the delightful Welsh styles and those created by early American settlers. Do not be too ambitious about size – better a cushion cover you can actually use than a quarter of a bedspread that never gets finished.

Once you start on crafts for your home, the list is almost endless. You name it and there is a class in it. Here are just a few – rug-making, picture framing, enamelling, pottery, mosaics, macramé, making lampshades – including some for those interestingly-shaped wine bottles which you have always intended to make into lamps. The fittings for these, by the way, can be obtained from most craft shops.

COOKERY

One subject that virtually everyone is interested in is cooking. Have you ever wished you were a better cook – not in every sphere but in one where you have the least success? Evening or daytime classes can give a lift to your pastry, or the courage to have a go at more exotic dishes than pizza and chips. A number of men have a flair for cooking and a couple who enjoy their meals could take it in turn to attend classes on different aspects of the subject – e.g. soufflés in the afternoon and Chinese regional cooking in the evening.

THE FAMILY TREE

As you get older you tend to remember more of your past, especially the things that happened when you were a youngster and what your grandparents told you about their own childhood. In our 70s, some of our favourite reading is about the 1930s – our own teens and early 20s. Often it is this interest which sparks off another hobby: genealogy. Tracing your family tree can be taken quite a way back before you need to call in outside help and it can become quite an absorbing hobby. As always, there are plenty of books on the subject. Although some people secretly hope for a bold bad Baron in their family tree, they are probably more likely to find English peasantry or yeoman stock with an intermingling of immigrant blood from Ireland or Scotland

PHOTOGRAPHY

There is a great deal of fun to be had from photography, even if you only use it for recording holiday scenes or family get-togethers and do not become involved in developing and enlarging.

Cameras are built around different film sizes. At the bottom of the size range are the little disc or very small 110-size film cameras. These are the only true pocket or handbag sizes, but the quality of the pictures is limited, so they can only be thought of as ultra-simple snapshot cameras.

Next up in size are the 35mm cameras which are the most popular. This is the size around which all the large-scale processing is geared. All the 'special offers' which drop through the letterbox are for this size of film.

Cameras using it range from a simple fixed-lens compact with several automatic features to a number of much more sophisticated types. Results with all these can be very good indeed.

Compacts and single-lens-reflex (SLR) cameras use the same size film – 35mm – but different types of viewfinder. The compact is a direct-vision finder, giving the same sort of view as the camera lens. It has one drawback which is that it may be difficult to frame nearby subjects as well. The SLR employs a pentaprism in the top of the camera and a mirror behind the lens to achieve very precise focusing and composition. With SLRs there are interchangeable lenses, but very few compacts provide for this. Really keen amateur photographers are inclined to use SLRs, whereas someone who merely wants a higher quality than the very tiny cameras will probably opt for a compact. Of these, the simpler and cheaper are as easy to use as any point-and-click camera, while the more sophisticated ones cost more but offer nearly as much scope as a single lens reflex.

The largest size film used by amateurs is 2¼ inches square, frequently chosen by professionals. If you have any ambitions about selling the occasional shot, check through *Writers' and Artists' Yearbook* first. Many magazines still insist on 2¼ inches as the minimum for reproduction, although some journals now indicate that they will be willing to accept 35mm.

The majority of enthusiasts have their film developed by either the high-street shops or the mail-order processors, but if one of your retirement hobbies is to be photography, then you will want to look into the subject of enlargers and dark-room equipment. It pays to weigh up costs carefully. Some photographers develop their own black-and-whites, sending the colour films to a processor, because they argue that costs are not all that different in the latter case. On the other hand, if you propose to do a good deal of colour photography and want to enlarge only a part of the picture, or to experiment with trick shots or try out the effects of different filters, then a combined colour and black-and-white enlarger could be the answer.

Like modelling, photography does not need a great deal of space in the home. We have seen darkrooms made from an understair cupboard, the partitioned-off end of a large Victorian bathroom, or an extension built on to the dining room. What is needed is an even temperature, which cuts out the average garden shed, access to running water and total darkness during certain stages of the work. A table top plus sufficient drawers and cupboards for photographic gear are also required.

Photography often starts as a spin off from another hobby. You may want to take pictures of a railway layout or a military diorama in the process of construction, or to record your garden at different times of the year. You may also want to photograph period architecture which can be modelled as part of a layout, adapting existing kits or making up from scratch. Photography can also be a useful tool for someone who decides to take up painting as a hobby, as a library of prints – trees, buildings, landscapes, animals or human figures – can be built up.

MAKING A PROFIT FROM YOUR HOBBY

Looking around an exhibition some years ago, we spotted a fine reproduction desk in burr walnut. The matching of the veneers was first rate, the design completely authentic, and the backs and undersides of the drawers as well finished as the fronts. When we remarked on it, we were told: 'That was done by a retired Army Colonel. When he had about a year to go before retiring, he applied to this furniture college for a three-year course. As soon as he left the Army he came here and by the end of the course his work was up to this sort of standard. We could sell anything he makes, but he only lets us have one or two pieces a year – the rest he makes for his wife, or for family and friends'.

This is not the only case of a hobby that could become a business. For many people this is their entry into a pleasant and profitable pastime, although there are others who shy away from making profit because it immediately takes the fun out of it and changes it from pleasure to work.

OUT AND ABOUT

There are very few hobbies that do not get you out of the home and provide a change of scene while you gather information about your particular interest. Sometimes this is incidental, but in other cases it is an essential part of the hobby. Anything that touches on natural history – the study of wild flowers, birds, butterflies and moths – will immediately get you out into the fresh air. So will an interest in the history of your locality. Before you have gone into it very deeply, you are visiting all the sites of historical interest, looking up information on listed buildings, and searching out maps of the locality at specialist shops. The latter may have to be done by mail, as these shops are limited in number.

Quite often one hobby leads to another: identifying local wild flowers can lead to rummaging through bric-a-brac shops for those dried flower pictures, popular before World War 1 and now enjoying a revival, or even to making these pictures or three-dimensional dried flower arrangements for yourself.

Unlike the Wodehouse character who every day knew 'less and less about more and more' in retirement, there is the opportunity to find out about anything that particularly interests you. Some people are interested in virtually anything. A couple we used to know enrolled every autumn at the evening institute we attended. They had started off with two subjects – art and the Albanian language and were steadily working their way through the alphabet. We often wondered if they ever reached zoology and Zen Buddhism.

Many hobbies can be learned for the first time, or your present standards can be improved by attending adult education courses, which are frequently available to pensioners at half-rates. Among the subjects offered are a wide range of crafts, collecting books, coins or stamps, natural history or history of your own locality, British wild flowers, birds and animals and musical appreciation.

In addition, there are a very wide variety of courses offered by private organisations, who can provide introductory literature on topics as far-ranging as amateur dramatics to brass rubbings or flower arranging to puppetry. It is very unlikely that, with all this choice available, a retired person will not be able to find one or more hobbies to interest him.

12 HOLIDAYS AND OUTINGS

While you are working full time, holidays have to be planned to fit in with those of your colleagues. You cannot always pick the time of year which you prefer. If you want to go further and stay away longer that is also not possible, because most firms have a stipulation that not more than, say 2 or 3 weeks can be taken at one time. It makes sense. If someone can be absent from his job for a longer time and it clearly makes very little difference, then management might be inclined to ask how necessary he was in the first place.

But when you retire, there is considerably more scope. A holiday can be planned for any time of the year and, in many instances, can be prolonged for a considerable period. If you have part-time work commitments, of course, these have to be honoured but, for the totally retired, the sky is the limit. The key factor is money.

Some people expect to cut down on holidays when they retire, even if while working they spent quite a high proportion of their income on the annual vacation. This is not at all necessary

If you take advantage of off-peak long-stay holidays with ultra-cheap flights and minimum prices for accommodation, you can practically break even with the cost of staying at home and shopping in your local stores. You are in a position to pick and choose. You avoid the overcrowded beaches, yet still have weather which is mild and sunny. You get more attention at the hotel, because there is not a large crowd all clamouring for meals at the same time.

The only thing to watch out for is that you have picked a place to stay where you are going to be happy for the next couple of months or so. To safeguard yourself, it is best to consult a publication called *The Agents'*

Hotel Gazetteer for the Resorts of Europe (from Continental Hotel Gazetteers). This is extremely frank about the hotels and pensions listed, so you can be warned in advance if the looked-forward-to holiday is likely to turn into a disaster.

CHOOSING A HOLIDAY

If you fancy a long-term cruising holiday, it is a good idea to take a short cruise first – a week or even a few days – to see if shipboard life is the life for you. Some people take to it with gusto, but others find that, although the food side is usually very well done, because they are more solitary individuals they are not attracted to the social life on board ship. In that case a berth on a much smaller vessel with only a few passengers might be the answer. But do not expect all the mod. cons of a luxury liner.

Your preference might be for a motoring holiday, if you enjoy driving; you can either take your own car or rent one when you arrive at the first European port. You can stop where you like and only drive as many kilometres in a day as you wish. You can splurge on a very ritzy meal one day and buy rolls and paté on the next. A number of tour companies offer a service of ferry and car-rental and it is not always necessary to come back to the point at which you picked up the car.

Caravans can also be hired in Channel ports when you arrive with your own car and this reduces the ferry charge. If you do a lot of caravanning, then you may wish to take your own caravan and all your equipment, having organised it so that everything is geared to your own taste. But for many people the hire service is a better choice. Camping carnets are required. These are available to members of the Automobile Association, Royal Automobile Club and the Camping and Caravan Club. Non-members can obtain these from the Great Britain Car Club, P.O. Box 11, Romsey, Hampshire S05 8XX. Much useful information is provided in *Caravan and Chalet Sites Guide*, obtainable from most bookshops.

Camp sites can be fairly simple or quite luxurious and the old idea of soggy sites with draughty tents or cramped caravans needs bringing up to date. Nor are you cut off from basic shopping needs or from entertainment and, if you enjoy the company of people of all ages, you will find a very good cross-section at most sites, from couples with young families to the middle-aged, and to people past retirement age.

Self-catering holidays have grown in popularity over the last few years. These are practical for family holidays, as anyone who has totted up the average day's expenditure on food and drink can corroborate. They are also well suited to retired couples. This is particularly true if one of them is not all that keen on foreign dishes, because you can buy your own food and cook it the way you like for some of the main meals and do your experimenting at the others.

Unless you want super luxury, you will find the villas or apartments provided by the well-known tour operators very comfortable and clean, and there is the bonus that your saving on hotel bills will allow you to give yourself plenty of treats in food and drink.

FLIGHTS

It is not surprising that many people get confused when looking through advertisements for holiday flights in the press. The cost of flights to the same place can differ by very large amounts and it is not easy at first glance to understand why.

Most very cheap flights are for bookings made a good while in advance or for the exact opposite – spur-of-the-moment flights only decided on a day or so before. It is very seldom necessary to pay the regular scheduled fares when going on holiday; in an emergency, yes, but not when you can either plan well ahead or just get up and go. Even on scheduled flights it is possible to get discount fares, such as the British Airways 'Pound-stretchers' or similar arrangements made by British Caledonian.

Look out for IPEX (instant purchase excursions) for last-minute bookings on a scheduled airline. These can be made as late as the afternoon of the day before you leave and are for specific flights out and back. In complete contrast are APEX and ABC fares – advance purchase excursions and advance booking charter. With these you do not have a chance to alter your leaving and return dates once they have been booked and generally you have to remain away for a minimum of 1 week. ABCs apply to charter travel and are bookable 3 to 6 weeks in advance. APEX are for scheduled airlines and have to be bought between 3 and 12 weeks in advance. In both cases you need to insure against missing the plane, otherwise you may not get your money back. (These are the arrangements at the time of writing this chapter, but they may vary from time to time, so it is necessary to check with your travel agent.) The Wakefield Fortune Group of travel agents publish a twice-yearly free leaflet called *A Plain Man's Guide to Air Fares* which helps a lot in understanding the extraordinary range of fares charged for flying you to the same place.

PACKAGE HOLIDAYS

If you still fancy going abroad, but like to leave someone else to do all the organising, a package tour is the obvious choice. You should be well catered for if you go to a reputable travel agent, and if the tour operators are members of the Association of British Travel Agents (ABTA). The tour operator has to have an ATOL number (air travel organiser's licence), so check that this is the position, if you want to be certain of compensation should anything go wrong. Be prepared for extras, whether they come in the form of surcharges for currency or fuel, airport charges or other supplements. It pays to add as much as 50 per cent to your budget to take care of all these eventualities.

MOTORING HOLIDAYS

Your choice may be for a motoring holiday abroad. If you are not already a member it is worthwhile taking out membership of either the AA or the RAC, both of which can provide really effective insurance for their members and also cover any passengers and the car itself. In addition, if you are to have carefree motoring, you can take out a policy to cover any mishaps in a specific country, e.g. Greece or Spain, through an insurance broker. A green card is required for both these countries and a bail bond is an additional requirement for Spain. The AA also supplies large red warning triangles in case of breakdown, as it is illegal to stop without one of these if you are driving on the Continent.

When to go can make a difference to the cost. Midweek-ferry prices cost less and it also pays to find out about any special offers and promotions. Petrol is cheaper in the UK, so it pays to fill up the car before you board the ferry. Finally, do not compete with yourself to see just how many kilometres you can cover in one day. There is no hurry. That is the whole point of a holiday touring by car. It seems a waste of time and money if you grip the wheel doggedly, as the landscape flashes by in a blur, just to be able to boast of the miles covered when you pack it in for the night. As in the UK, side roads give a much better idea of a country than motorways do, which lets you take your holiday more easily and get more out of it.

When coming back to the ferry port, if you've had quite a long drive say, up from the south of France – treat yourself to a bunk on the boat in order to get a good sleep before starting the drive from the UK port to your home.

MINI-BREAKS AND DAY TOURS

Sometimes the cash does not run to an annual holiday, but it is well worth seeing if you can trim the budget to allow a few days break. This type of vacation also suits the large number of people who get bored with a normal holiday, but are happy to take 3 or 4 days off here and there. Spaced around the year, these add up to a break every 3 or 4 months, and are just as beneficial as a full 2 or 3 weeks at one go.

As soon as Spring starts, the advertising of these mini-tours begins, and one of the most popular is a 3-day tour of the Dutch bulb fields. From then on, they continue right through the season, with offers of 5 days in Amsterdam, or of mid-week visits to Belgian or German beer and wine festivals. Travelling by sea and coach, these are some of the most economical breaks you can get.

Taking up very little time, and costing even less, are the day outings, both in the UK and across the Channel. Very popular are the 1-day visits to French Channel ports, with plenty of time to look around once you get off the ferry and to do your shopping at the supermarkets or in the local open-air market.

In the UK, the safari parks come high up in the list of places to visit. Drive-through game reserves, such as Woburn, Windsor and Longleat contain an incredible range and number of wild animals. At Bekesbourne near Canterbury there are caged and free-roaming animals, or you can go up to Stapleford Park in Leicestershire to see lions and leopards, monkeys and crocodiles. There are also a number of smaller wildlife parks featuring many specimens of European animals and birds, badgers and wild boar, wolves, otters and different types of fox.

At some of these places it is also possible to enjoy beautifully laid-out gardens, such as Savill Gardens in Windsor Great Park. Keen gardeners may like to pay a visit to the famous gardens of Sissinghurst Castle in Kent, where one of the most attractive features is a garden planted solely with grey-leaved, white-flowering plants. The Royal Horticultural Gardens at Ripley in Surrey are particularly fine in Spring, and the rose gardens at St Albans have a fantastic range of scent and colour later in the year. You can obtain a guide to the gardens of England and Wales which are open to the public. For details of famous houses, there is the AA *Guide to Stately Homes, Castles and Gardens in Britain*.

If you are a keen walker, one of the best ways of spending a day out is by taking part in a walk organised by the National Parks, where you not only see the local plants and animals but are given expert information about them as you go round. On nature trails you find your own way around, but descriptive labels identify plants and trees, while on farm trails there is a guided tour of buildings and farmland. Details of all these can be had from the Countryside Commission and the only major expenditure is the initial fare, assuming that you have a pair of really comfortable walking shoes and some sort of weather gear for the unexpected shower.

ACTIVITY HOLIDAYS

Growing in popularity are activity and study holidays and both the National Institute of Adult Education and the Central Bureau for Educational Visits and Exchanges give information on short residential courses held in very pleasant surroundings. You can take a holiday plus tuition in a number of subjects, including archaeology and painting. Adventure holidays, particularly in places such as the Aviemore Centre in Scotland, enable you to follow one or more interests. Some offer food and accommodation while others are self-catering and the prices generally cover all hiring of equipment plus tuition. An important point is that, if two of you are going, you can each follow your own interest, which could be archery, hill-walking, skating or ski-ing.

Holidays with a theme attract a number of people with hobbies. You have only to look through the classified advertisements in specialist magazines to see the scope provided. If your hobby is railways, you can ride on railway trains all over the world on special tours where you see locos and rolling stock currently used and can visit museums devoted to those of the past.

For golfers, there are tours which take in various countries and allow for the fact that your spouse may not be a golfer and provide alternative entertainment for her/him.

Anglers, divers and keen swimmers can all head off, alone or in shoals, to rivers and harbours and, if you enjoy sailing but have never spent a week on the Norfolk Broads, then you have missed a lot.

Photographers are also well catered for. The photographic magazines contain advertisements for guided or go-as-you-please tours, and the reduction on group travel allows you to spend more on films and filters.

Gardeners, as already pointed out, have an enormous range of famous gardens to visit and gloat over, and at some of these it is possible to buy plants grown on the premises.

There is hardly a weekend during the summer months when there is not some event organised by local clubs (aero, boat, rail), or a rally of veteran or vintage cars, commercial vehicles, tractors or fairground engines. Many of these are easily accessible, either by car or by public transport.

If you are new to an area and want to get to know people quickly, a very good way is by attending local fetes. Many of these run stalls staffed, for example, by members of the area's historical society or the local ecology group and there are, of course, the branches of the Women's Institute and Red Cross, as well as groups associated with local churches.

CONCESSIONS
Both in the UK and in certain European countries there are many opportunities of reduced-price travel for the over-60s and these have been discussed in Chapter 6.

These special offers add up to a considerable saving in cost of travel for those over retirement age. As many of them vary from time to time, it is always worth checking that you are getting the cheapest possible fare available.

There are also facilities at British holiday resorts where pensioners can pay reduced rates for entertainment and so on, if they show a pension book. Enquiries can be made at tourist boards, information centres or town halls. If you do not have a book because your pension is paid directly into a bank, it is a good idea to apply for a special card showing your entitlement to reductions, which is supplied free by the Department of Health and Social Security, Central Pensions Branch (FW), Newcastle-on-Tyne, NR98 1YX.

PREPARING FOR YOUR HOLIDAY
Some weeks before taking a holiday in a country which you have not visited before, make a point of reading about it in your local library. It is always a bit of a let-down to return home and find that you have missed the chance of seeing something unique which has only been a short distance from your holiday apartment.

Guides vary, but among very reliable sources of information are the Berlitz *Travel Guides*, A. & C. Black's *Blue Guides* and Collins' *Companion Guides*. For the UK there are also the *Visitor's Guides* published by Moorland. Prices of guides vary a great deal and you can save by reading up as much as you can at the library and then investing in an inexpensive pocket guide for sightseeing.

People often tend to go to extremes when planning health precautions on holiday. If you have chosen a holiday at one or more places in Europe, or in the Middle East or North Africa, you can check with the high-street chemist at home in case malaria preventatives are needed. In any case, you will need tablets for the inevitable tummy upsets. In a hot summer, such tablets are also a must for holidays in the UK, as well as medicine for mild indigestion or a sudden summer cold. Activity holidays require a corner in the suitcase for a small bottle of antiseptic and a supply of dressings for grazes or blisters. On all holidays, if you are a natural target for every type of winged or crawling insect, pack a cream or spray to act as a deterrent.

As regards clothes, we have always believed in travelling light. The minimum of clothes in your luggage allows space for holiday souvenirs and can be sufficient to cover all eventualities if you stick to non-iron drip-dry fabrics. With comfortable shoes or sandals, a hat that shades the back of your neck, a lightweight roll-up mac and a pullover or cardigan for cool evenings, you should be off to the start of an enjoyable holiday.

It goes without saying that, if going out of the UK, you are well advised to be covered with extra insurance for sickness and accident, on top of what the tour operator or the airline provides. If you are well covered, you do not have to try to find a way through the confusing bureaucratic forms, trying to discover which countries do or do not have reciprocal agreements with the UK or, in the case of those who do, whether medicines have to be paid for even if hospitalisation is free. Also, it pays to time your dental check-up shortly before you go, rather than to cope with toothache during your vacation.

HOME EXCHANGE

There is one other way of cutting the cost of holidays which has an appeal for the more relaxed or more adventurous. This is the home-swap, which is still a minority type of holiday, but rapidly growing. You can arrange this through friends or go to one of the agencies doing these exchanges. The cost of the holiday is then limited to the air fare (if going abroad) and any outings you have while there.

There are those who would be horrified at the idea of strangers using their home, but a large number of people are not at all worried and cite the advantages of each family having everything laid on in a domestic rather than a hotel atmosphere.

To do it without any hassles later, it is essential to be businesslike about the arrangements. The agencies handling this type of exchange do not take responsibility in any way once they have added your name to the list of willing swappers and given you particulars of your opposite numbers. So, to start off, you need to exchange references, especially bank references, to get electricity and gas meters read and billed immediately before you set off on holiday, and to get your exchanger to do the same. This applies even more to telephone bills. Both parties should be prepared to pay a worthwhile deposit (which can be held by a bank or lawyer) against possible claims under these three headings. Clear up any insurance problems by getting your own insurance company to continue to give insurance cover during the swap and get the other family to do the same at their end.

With these sensible precautions, there is no reason why both families should not have a very good holiday – and for a very reasonable outlay.

13 ANIMALS AS COMPANIONS

One thing that people miss most when they retire is companionship. They have had the company of their colleagues at office, factory or shop. Even if they have worked on their own, e.g. as a sales representative, they have had regular customers to talk to with whom they have become friends. If they have run a shop, restaurant or club, again there have been 'regulars', people whom they knew by sight and by name.

It may sound idyllic to retire to your own home and potter about all day. But the day can be very long. And the nights are even longer. Those who retire unwillingly are especially hard-hit. They do not want to be segregated among others whom they regard as finished and who have no interest for them or in them. Understandably this affects people who take early retirement more than those who are quite relieved at giving up going out daily to work. But it also affects people of any age who have had a very active life or a job that brought them into contact with many people.

One lady of 80 was invited to join an old people's club when she retired from running a busy pub. She scorned the idea and told the social worker to ask 'the old girl upstairs'. (The lady in the upper flat was a mere stripling of 65.) In fact, the 80-year-old would have enjoyed the OAPs' club, which included many equally live pensioners among its members. But what she was trying to say was that she did not want to mix just with her own age-group. She had always mixed with all ages and types of people and that was what she preferred.

In Chapters 9 and 10 we discussed paid and unpaid work on retirement. There is no better way of meeting people than through work – paid part-time occupation or voluntary effort. It is not just meeting people but meeting those with whom you have something in common. There is no more reason to suppose that a pensioner will get on with another of the same age because both are pensioners than to suppose that every teenager will like other teenagers on sight.

The one thing that does not work is to go out looking for companionship without first finding out whether you will have anything to say to each other when you do meet. You can discover this by joining a group, which could be a local allotment society, one of the many groups run by churches in the area, or any of the voluntary organisations mentioned in Chapter 10. Once in, you can sort out how you can play a part and find out which people you will hit it off with and which it is best for you to avoid as much as possible.

DOGS

One of the easiest ways of making acquaintances is when walking a dog. This brings us to one of the best forms of companionship, which is to own a pet. Any down-to-earth vet will testify to the value of companion animals and the old-style family doctor was equally aware of it. It is not always possible to keep a pet when you are out at work because the animal should not be left on its own all day. But when you retire there is the opportunity to have a pet and to enjoy its company for as many hours in the day as you wish.

Dogs come high on the list of companion animals when people retire. There may be a dog already, in the case of a married couple where the wife does not have a job, works part-time or occasionally, but if you are on your own, or both work full-time, there is no scope for dog ownership. The self-employed have the advantage that they can call the shots on this. Pubs have always had a tradition of keeping dogs and, in these days, a dog kept by a shop proprietor can be the very best form of burglar deterrent. When we had a model shop, our two German Shepherds, Amos and Susi, were not only good watchdogs but were very friendly companions to us and to the customers. Inevitably in that time there were a few incidents, when louts came in looking for easy pickings. The sight of the male dog emerging from the back room had an instant effect and they would quickly remember an appointment elsewhere. The bitch had an uncanny knack of telling when a dud cheque was being offered. She only growled three times at customers and, in each case, their cheques came bouncing back. Presumably she sensed their unease. To a dog the scent of a scared person is probably disturbing.

As a rule, people are inclined to continue with one breed of dog rather

133

than to switch from large to small or smooth to shaggy. If the family starts off with a golden retriever pup for the children, the odds are that from then on each dog they have will be the same breed. We had never owned our own dog until we were over 50, but some of my husband's family had bred and owned German Shepherd dogs. So it was inevitable that, when we chose a dog ourselves, it should be one of that breed.

If you are thinking of buying a dog as a companion in your retirement, there are a few points to be considered. There is the cost of buying and the expense in keeping the dog, including veterinary fees. There is the amount of exercise needed by different breeds. There is also the question of moulting; some do it a lot and some scarcely moult at all. Then there is the question of whether to keep a dog or a bitch. Finally, there is the matter of the dog's age – should it be a pup or a fully grown animal?

We shall consider these points one by one. If you are in your 50s you are likely to be active enough to cope with a puppy's training. If you are in your late 60s or 70s then you have to consider whether it is fair to take on an animal which is very young and almost bursting with health. Your capacity for exercise may be a short stroll twice a day – weather permitting – but even pups, which should not be over-exercised, need more than that.

If money is not such a problem and you are fit and looking forward to training a pup, then it is wise to buy from a reputable breeder. In the UK, names of breeders who specialise in certain breeds, can be obtained from the Kennel Club. You can, of course, buy from friends whose bitch has had a litter, but you should obtain the pedigree Kennel Club certificate for both the sire and dam.

If you would prefer to provide a home for an older rescued dog, or one needing to be rehoused due to its owner's death, then you can contact the RSPCA or other animal organisations such as the Dumb Friends League. If in London, there is, of course, the Battersea Dogs' Home (which, incidentally, also deals with cats). The charges are pitched very low compared with the cost of buying a pedigree pup from a breeder and you have the satisfaction of providing a home for a dog badly in need of one. However, you should bear in mind that a grown dog with an unknown background may have bad habits which you may not be able to break easily.

The cost of feeding varies quite a lot, depending on the size of the dog. Not all large dogs are big feeders. Our own German Shepherds and a friend's Jack Russell ate about the same amount, yet Great Danes we know have all had big appetites. We have always given our dogs a combination of cooked and canned meats, together with the granules sold by petshops and by most supermarkets, as well as liver once a week, an occasional raw egg yolk and, as rewards, small cubes of Cheddar cheese. (I had a bad habit of giving sweet biscuits to our bitch, at one time, but having to restrict her food because she put on weight cured me of that. A bitch on a diet is like a human being on a diet – a pain in the neck.)

Some butchers keep a tray of scraps for pets, which helps to keep down the cost of feeding, but we have never found the various forms of pet mince much help because generally they are far too fatty. On the other hand, for an old dog, the slabs of pet-meats (chicken, turkey etc.) from petshops, appear to be more easily digested. Fresh water, frequently changed and given in a clean bowl, is needed every day, but milk is not an essential part of a dog's diet once puppyhood has passed. All the same, quite a number of dogs enjoy a bowl of tea, and three out of four of those we have owned have done so. It is impossible to give exact costs of feeding, but as a guestimate we would say allow about one-quarter to one-third of what you reckon for yourself. It is totally unfair that petfoods should carry VAT in the UK and even more so that the vet's charges should be subject to the same tax.

A vet's training is very long and expensive; all drugs prescribed have to be paid for by the client, and there is the imposition of VAT on top of this. Veterinary fees might well deter some people from owning a pet, but there are two ideas which help. The first is the growing practice of taking out insurance for the animal. Generally this amounts to quite a low annual premium in return for treatment whenever necessary. Usually there is a clause excluding the first visit of a series, and most policies do not cover a dog beyond the age of 8 years. Third-party risks are also covered, so that if a dog causes an accident you are insured against this. Policies vary from company to company and it is wise to look at several before deciding which one to take out.

The other way of dealing with animal sickness or injury is to find the nearest branch of the PDSA (People's Dispensary for Sick Animals) in your locality. All essential treatments are provided free if the owner cannot afford payment, but if you can manage something towards the cost, you are invited to contribute what you can. There are branches of the PDSA in every major town and, in addition, there are mobile units which provide treatment. Details can be obtained from local libraries or petshops.

Dogs vary considerably in the amount of exercise needed. Up to a point the larger breeds need more, but this does not apply so much to the very large ones. A St Bernard and some Great Danes are happy with far less exercise than the active breeds, such as German Shepherds, Boxers and Dobermans. Every dog needs regular exercise, which means not just a walk on a lead but the chance to run about and play off the lead. Before deciding what type of dog to get, have a look at the accessibility of local parks and open spaces and visualise the walk to reach them when carried out on a bitterly cold, wet day. If you are fortunate enough to have a large garden, this does help, but the dog still needs to go out, to meet other people and other dogs. The worst thing that can happen to a dog, apart from downright ill-treatment, is to keep it shut up in a house or flat.

All dogs require daily grooming with a brush. In urban areas, it is wise to examine their paws whenever they come back after a walk, to see if there are any cuts due to broken glass or jagged-edged cans left around by vandals, or bits of grit from road-surfacing. If moulting worries you, go for a breed that does little or no moulting, e.g. Doberman, Boxer, Short-Haired Dachshund. We taught our Alsatian bitch to let us run the nozzle of the cylinder-type vacuum cleaner over her when she was in full moult. So long as it did not come near her face or ears she was quite content, and it saved vacuuming the carpet.

A dog or a bitch? That is entirely a matter of preference. A bitch is less likely to get into scraps and, if spayed, you don't have the problem of followers. But a friendly, good-tempered male is an equally good choice and we never had any problems with the three that we have owned. The only minor problem we sometimes experienced was with the type of immature young man who equated owning a large dog with a macho image, and encouraged his animal to pick fights with other large dogs. If you are worried about that, opt for a bitch. It is rare for a male dog to pick on a bitch – which distinguishes dogs from human beings.

At present, the UK regulation is that the owner must take out a licence when the puppy is over the age of 6 months, and keep it up to date annually. The law also requires that dogs wear a collar with their address on it. Apart from being the law, this is a wise provision. Anyone whose dog has gone missing, even for a short time, knows what a tense time it is until the animal is found, so any means of finding and identifying becomes absolutely vital.

CATS

Singly or in varying numbers, cats have always been popular pets. In great-grandpa's day they were usually thought of as catchers of rats and mice. But even so, there was generally one smooth character who soon acquired the status of a fireside pet, who became the cat-on-the-mat and all that went with it. A cat is an ideal pet where garden space is limited and the owner also does not want to exercise an animal. They are also easy to house-train. In fact, most kittens sold are already house-trained and, if not, can quickly be taught to go out and scratch in the garden or to use a litter tray indoors.

Contrary to the traditional idea of the cat being a fish-eater, apart from what it caught in the way of mice and birds, many cats are not all that keen on fish, though the majority like a diet which includes both meat and fish. Meat can be given cooked or raw, minced or chopped up small, but if you start with raw meat the cat is not likely to fancy the cooked variety and vice versa. There are exceptions. Our two cats preferred cooked food but made an exception in the case of liver, which was always eaten raw. Incidentally, one of our dogs was a keen fish-eater, especially if the fish was kippers or pilchards. And every animal we have owned has never refused sardines. Whether for cats or dogs, fish should always be carefully boned, and the same applies to meats such as rabbit or chicken.

Cats, with few exceptions, groom themselves but need twice-weekly brushing to get rid of loose hairs in case of the short-haired varieties, and once-daily for long haired types. But both kinds need daily brushing during the moulting period.

Cats and dogs, however well looked after, can pick up fleas, particularly during the warmer months. These are easily coped with by using a proprietary insect powder or spray, keeping it clear of the animal's eyes. Any box or basket should be treated. Carpets and upholstered furniture also need occasional treatment and any blanket or rug should be washed frequently. Dogs can enjoy a bath occasionally – we have always used the hose to give the dogs their baths in the garden, where they can shake themselves without flooding the house. Set the temperature at tepid and watch it stays that way. Smaller dogs can be bathed inside a plastic bath placed on a towel inside your own bath. The towel protects the bath surface and also gives them a foothold if they get out of the plastic bath. Alternatively, they can be hosed down in the garden in the same way as larger dogs. Some cats do not mind being bathed and, if they have taken to this while young, you can save yourself a lot of work. As with flea sprays, watch out for eyes and ears while shampooing or rinsing.

BIRDS

If, when retired, you are living in a flat where cats or dogs are not permitted, you might like to consider buying a canary or budgerigar. They are extremely good company for someone living alone, and the amount of work involved can be quite light if you follow a set routine for cage-cleaning and for sweeping up any husks or seeds on the floor around the cage. If you have never owned a bird before, buy one of the inexpensive books stocked by petshops, which contain advice on the type of cage and on food and drink that is suitable.

Canaries need a cage at least 16 inches long and with a height a little less; they should be shielded from damp and draughts, out of the reach of any cats. It should not be hung in a window or any sunny spot in the room. Proprietary mixed seeds, stored in an airtight tin or glass jar, are their basic food, with greenstuff such as watercress, dandelion leaves, lettuce (all washed and dried) hung from the top of the cage. Any stale vegetables should be removed when cleaning. Canaries also like some grit, which can be placed in a small container in one corner of the cage, and there should be fresh water as well as a separate plastic bowl for bathing.

Budgerigars need cages as large as possible and, like the canary, should be kept away from draught, cats and strong sun. However, on warm days, the cage can be put out of doors in the shade, though you will need to watch out all the time for cats. Fresh water is required and a cuttlefish bone for keeping the beak in trim, plus washed green vegetables as for canaries. In case of budgies, groundsel should also be given. Indoors they can be let out of the cage, provided all doors and windows are closed. If you want one to talk, do not expect it to learn quickly. Take things very slowly, teaching the bird a few simple phrases, and by 3 or 4 months of age it will probably have picked up some of these.

If you become concerned about excessive moult or listlessness in canaries, they can be taken to the vet or the PDSA for treatment with suitable drugs. It may also be necessary for budgerigars to have the beak trimmed and the claws clipped from time to time.

SMALL RODENTS

Small furry animals, such as hamsters, guinea pigs or cavies, also make friendly and affectionate pets. If kept in a suitable house, with dry clean litter, they are extremely clean and have no odour. All thrive in a normal room temperature of around 60-70°F. Hamsters are particularly active in the evening and night-time, and gerbils have bouts of activity throughout the whole 24 hours, so both are good pets for people who suffer from insomnia. All three types are easy to feed if you follow the instructions given in the inexpensive little books sold by most petshops, and all have a lifespan of some 3 years.

While hamsters are loners, guinea pigs enjoy the company of others, e.g. one male to one or more females, and gerbils like to live in pairs – two of the same sex or a male and female.

FISH

The only problem with keeping fish is that you can very quickly become hooked on wanting a bigger and bigger aquarium. Setting up a fish tank is obviously more expensive than buying a small animal and cage, but it can be a fascinating occupation. Aquaria have become a feature of dentists' waiting rooms and are also to be found in the foyers of some large firms, because they are not only decorative but also very relaxing.

If you become an aquarist, you will need to buy some fairly expensive equipment to begin with, but after that it is quite cheap to maintain the tank and keep the fish in good condition. A specialist shop will advise on the types of fish which will live together peacefully in a community tank. If you have knowledgeable friends, get them to go with you to pick out the right tank and suitable fish. If it is a cold-water tank (around 60°F), you can have a good variety, including the popular and less well-known types of goldfish, shubunkin and koi carp. If going in for tropical fish, which need a temperature of about 72-78°F, an automatic heater with thermostat will be required, plus a thermometer for regular temperature checks, especially in the event of power cuts. The tank should be lit from above, to reproduce the effect of sun shining on a pool or stream. The specialist shop can also supply plants, gravel or sand for their roots, and rocks. If you propose to keep a number of fish, an air pump and filter will also be needed.

One common mistake is overcrowding and another is overfeeding. A few pinches of food once or twice a day is all that is needed. A catfish is a natural scavenger, so include one of these to help keep the tank clean.

COMMITMENT

Some people hesitate to buy a pet because they do not want to be tied down. They like to go away when and where they wish, without having to make arrangements for a pet.

If they go away a great deal, they would be better off without a bird or animal, but if it is only a matter of the occasional holiday or visit there is no great difficulty in organising for these. An aquarium can be looked after by a friend or neighbour with very little trouble – just a daily visit – and most petshops will take over birds and tiny animals for a small charge. Not all cats and dogs take well to boarding, but it is possible for a friend to feed the cat in your absence and generally to keep an eye on it. If you have installed a cat flap there is no problem about access, but a cat kept in an upper flat would need to be let out for exercise, so it might be easier for a friend to move into your place during absence.

That would also be necessary where a dog is kept, unless you can take it away with you. Obviously, that is not possible if you are having a holiday abroad, and you will need to consider boarding kennels, asking a friend or member of the family to take over the flat temporarily, or engaging a homesitter. If you decide on kennels, try to get a recommendation from another dog-owner, or from your vet. Kennels vary considerably and you will want to know that your dog is being well looked after in your absence.

ADVANTAGES OF PET OWNERSHIP

Why do people keep pets? One reason frequently given is that they make you laugh or smile. This applies especially to dogs. As Samuel Butler said: 'The great pleasure of a dog is that you may make a fool of yourself with him, and not only will he not scold you, but he will make a fool of himself too'.

Having a pet to look after is an incentive to establish a routine, which is important for people living alone, who can easily get into the habit of skipping meals or forgetting to keep up with any medication prescribed. They are less likely to do so if there is an animal to be fed, groomed and exercised. Another point is that when you go out on your own for a while, you do not come back to an empty house, but to an uncritical welcome and a display of affection.

Science is at last coming round to the view that companion animals play a useful role in providing enjoyment for people who live in various types of institution, including retirement homes. An organisation named 'Pro-Dogs' initiated year-round visits by members' dogs to a number of institutions, with very good results in improvement in health and morale of the residents. Dogs have to be checked for suitable temperament and a wide range of breeds qualify. The visits need to be made on a regular basis, because residents look forward to them a great deal as they get to know the animals.

Not all sheltered-housing developments allow people to bring their pets with them, so if you are investigating these, check up on this to avoid distress. A helpful guide to sheltered housing is issued by Age Concern and the National Housing and Town Planning Council. This points out that, normally, it is necessary to obtain written permission from the management organisation before bringing in a pet. So, before taking any final step, check the attitude towards this matter.

Even if it becomes impossible to own any form of pet, do not overlook the enjoyment to be derived from watching wildlife. A kitchen or living room with windows overlooking a garden will provide views of a wide variety of birds. It is very pleasant if you can coax some of the bolder varieties to come to the sill for food. With more countryside animals coming into the town it is not uncommon to see squirrels, hedgehogs or even the urban fox from time to time.

14 MAKE IT EASY
FOR YOURSELF

The time to plan so as to make life easy for yourself is before you need to do so. Do not wait until you are forced to call on others for help because you find it difficult to do many of the simple tasks that you now take for granted.

Here are some ideas which let you go it alone. Retired people are often reluctant to call in assistance and will go without rather than summon it. If you get organised, there are many ways of making things easy for yourself and avoiding the need for any outside help.

You may have had an accident that leads to a temporary disablement, but want to feel independent while you are recovering. Two useful aids are a handle each side of the bath, to make getting in and out easier, and another handle on the wall by the lavatory. An additional boon can be a floor-to-ceiling rail, fixed just outside the bath, which you can hold on to as you get in and out. Even easier is a reclining bath with a side-opening door, specially designed for the very elderly or disabled. This can be used by other members of the household and eliminates all problems of entry and exit.

If you have lost the use of one hand, e.g. through a stroke or arthritis, the occupational-therapy department of the local hospital will be able to help regarding gadgets suited to your problem. These include gadgets which assist in peeling vegetables, eating and washing-up, as well as dressing and undressing.

Do you find it difficult to open a tightly-fitting jam-jar lid? Try one of these methods
1. A wide elastic band round the edge will help to give a firmer grip. Snap it on and twist the lid.

2. Use a bone-handled knife to tap round the lid to break the vacuum so that less effort is needed to open it. Only that type of knife will do the trick.
3. Press down the lid with a piece of foam rubber before turning.
4. Slip on a leather or strong plastic glove – not a woollen one – and give the lid another twist.

Alternatively, buy a special jar/bottle opener. This adjusts to the circumference of the lid or bottle top and a gentle twist will quickly remove it.

Dropping a needle on the floor when you cannot bend down to pick it up can be an annoyance. So can trying to reach a book on an upper shelf. There are special reaching aids which enable you to get hold of what you want, whether it is on a shelf, the floor or a table. They can be used when you are in a chair or even in bed. A magnetic tip takes care of the dropped needle problem.

Are you having difficulty in coping with very tiny parts when mending a watch or doing very fine embroidery, or when assembling or painting a model? An adjustable magnifying glass which hangs on a cord round the neck leaves both hands free to get on with your hobby.

Someone with backache often finds it difficult to put on socks, stockings or tights. One gadget involves putting the sock or stocking over the concave side of a plastic device, sliding the foot inside and pulling up with attached tapes.

One of the hardest jobs is to remove boots or wellies. If you do not have a stately valet, one answer could be a boot/shoe remover that eliminates stooping. A strongly-built platform with a notch to anchor the heel, lets you remove the footwear easily. A very long-handled shoehorn will do the same job for your shoes.

Shopping trolleys are a familiar sight in most high streets, but a surprisingly large number of old people still burden themselves with a heavy carrier bag in each hand instead of buying a trolley which will make shopping easier. If you do not overload them, these trolleys will last for years. At one time it was worth buying the best and most sturdily-built type but, for a household of only one or two, a lightweight, cheaper model is more suitable. These are easier to put in a car boot or into a railway carriage and, on buses, have the advantage of taking up less space. Whichever type you choose, very few shops sell replacement bags, but as these tend to last as long as the lighter-weight frames, this is another reason for selecting one of this type.

Instead of the traditional gold watch, a far more useful retirement present would be a fully reclining chair, with back-and-foot tilting and an optional high seat. Another welcome gift would be an adjustable bed that works automatically to raise one or both feet or prop up your back. This is by no means cheap, but can provide hours of comfort and increase the chance of a good night's sleep for people with respiratory, circulatory or arthritic problems.

If you are prone to forget where you put important papers, why not use retirement as a chance to get organised? Instead of stuffing them behind ornaments on the sideboard, house them in a lockable metal box that contains labelled folders for everything you do not want to mislay – insurance policies, birth and marriage certificates, passport, will, income tax papers, as well as all the documents for the car plus guarantees, or instruction books for household appliances. Such a box takes up very little space, is fire-resistant, and means an end to scrabbling through handbag or pockets before you eventually find what you are looking for – if you are lucky!

When people get older they find crowded stores and parking difficulties a deterrent to shopping. Even if they face them, there is still the fact that the store does not deliver or that there is a sizable charge to be reckoned on, on top of the price. Mail-order catalogues can then prove extremely useful. Most include a number of lines well suited to the retired such as bed or lap tray-tables, cushions shaped to wedge under the knees or in the small of the back, folding walking-sticks, needle threaders and a variety of draught excluders. Particularly useful is sponge-rubber tubing that fits over such items as nail-files, toothbrushes, or potato-peelers which are difficult to grip.

Many ideas save effort and do not cost money. One we have discovered at first hand is to use a colander when peeling vegetables. Instead of chasing pieces of carrot or turnip around a plastic bowl or sink when you have finished the job, they are all inside the colander and can be emptied on to the compost heap or put in a plastic bag ready for the dustbin if you do not have a garden.

A colander or wire basket can be placed inside a saucepan or chip pan to hold vegetables. When cooked, you lift the colander clear and empty away the boiling water.

To save bending, fix the kitchen waste-bin a couple of feet above floor level. If space is too limited to allow for a bin, make use of plastic carrier bags hung from a hook at the same height. When full, you simply tie a knot in the top of the bag, ready for the dustbin, and replace it with a fresh one.

15 CASE HISTORIES

Here, we include some examples of people who have shown an adventurous spirit in getting ready for retirement before the actual date arrived. Others have taken up some entirely new undertaking or launched out in a completely different way, even though they were in receipt of a pension and could take things easily.

FRANCIS AND ANNA COLLINS – EXPATRIATES

Francis Collins says: 'Until I reached the age of 63, I thought very little about the problem of retirement. I gave advice to others on the subject but as a sole practising accountant, I never had time to devote to my own affairs.

'The first three years of building up the practice left me with an overdraft which remained until I retired. Curiously enough, by the time I was 63 I was enjoying a relatively high income, coupled with a large overdraft and an uncomfortable mortgage. My wife Anna and I then decided to work really hard for a further five years in order to clear our debts. Needless to say, this was useless. At 65 I was getting very tired, and so began to contemplate ways of retiring fully or partially.

'Fevered sums scribbled on scrap paper convinced me that I would have to sell up, move to a smaller house, and carry on a reduced practice for ever.

'Then suddenly everything came together. Someone wanted to buy my practice. I found a property in France at a price which, if I sold up in England at a good price, would provide us with a modest but sufficient income to enable us to enjoy our remaining years halfway up a mountain in a very beautiful part of France.

'We decided to take a chance. The house sold at our asking price, which was way beyond estimates given to us by estate agents; the practice sold reasonably well, and suddenly we had a 240-year-old house in France and our debts were all paid.

'Next came a period of trying to arrange the coincidence of leaving our home, completing all the necessary paperwork so as to obtain visas, papers for the cat and dog, arranging for storage and removal of our furniture to France, clearing up work-in-progress of the practice and helping my successor to get to know the clients and to find his feet. In the middle of all this, I had to go into hospital for an operation. The visas took a dreary long time, so long in fact that we almost gave up. By now we were living with friends and are eternally grateful to them for putting up with us for two months instead of the fortnight that had been thought sufficient.

'Why did we wish to retire to France? First, Anna speaks the language fluently and has visited France a number of times in order to teach English to business people. We had always noticed that her health generally seemed much better when she was in a drier climate, and so we thought that to live in the lower Alps would be helpful. Also, I know the country fairly well, having spent many holidays with French friends. I do not speak more than a few words or phrases but am quite confident that in a year I will manage quite well. Again, I wanted to get away from it all, to uncomplicate my life as much as possible. I had had too much worry and pressure from people and events for too long. Having to keep up to date with changes in taxation and law had become a burden, and I felt that the only way out was to run somewhere which would allow me to lose touch as soon as possible.

'In the event, a small amount of translation of business forms or advertising material has started to come my way, which occupies quite a lot of time delving in dictionaries to elucidate the exact meanings.

'Having bought an old property, we have much home decorating and improvements to do which should take a year or so. The garden is small, but needs much sweat and toil before it becomes a simple job to maintain.

'Although there is a certain amount of standardisation developing within the European Community, there are still very big differences between France and England. The currency takes a long time to comprehend sufficiently to be able to think in terms of translating back into sterling all the time. Bureaucracy is another area where the French have many interesting, and initially disconcerting, differences from the

English. Manners and conventions are very different, particularly when one moves to a farming area in the middle or southern part of that country. I also have the problem of making myself understood and, conversely, understanding others, and many weird results can arise from the inability to communicate. My wife has not got this problem, but I frequently make extraordinary statements or misinterpret questions and answers.

'Before we moved to France I tried to calculate how the cost of living varied between the two countries, and I have now nearly completed a table of our costs in France, but this must be given a little extra time so that unusual highs and lows can be ironed out.

EDNA MARTIN – HOMESITTER

Edna Martin, still in her 50s, first came across the idea of homesitting when she read a paragraph in the *Observer* newspaper about an agency called Homesitters. She found the idea strange but rather intriguing and, as a telephone number was given, rang up to find out what it was all about. Since then she has stayed at a number of homes while their owners have gone away. Unlike many sitters, whose spouses are retired and who spend the whole day together at the various homes, Edna's husband is still working. Instead of catching his regular train home each evening, for a number of weeks in the year he now takes a ticket to someone else's home. As he works in London she takes on 'sits' all within easy reach of the capital.

She says: 'In doing this work we have become part of so many different places, and have acquired a huge 'family' of animals. This is particularly so when the home-owner asks for the same sitter again and they are able to renew acquaintance with the house and family and the various pets.

'You take over completely from the householder, find out the routine absolutely to the letter, so that everything goes smoothly. If the decorators are coming in to do up the living room during the day, you deal with them just as if it was your own home'.

That is the key to successful home-minding. As she says: 'You need to be a very caring person with a strong sense of responsibility. You are constantly thinking: 'This is what I would want done if it were my own home'.

Sitters do not have to do any gardening but most of them would cut the lawns and water the plants. She recalls: 'At one house there were about a hundred pots indoors, and several hundred other pot-plants outside. You would naturally want to see that they were watered and kept in good condition until the owners got back'.

Sometimes an elderly relative may remain in the house if they do not wish to accompany the family on holiday or go to stay with friends. In that case, the sitter is introduced to them beforehand and there is the chance to have a cup of tea and a chat, or a meal together, to get to know each other. She thinks it is easier for singles or couples without ties and that homesitting is a very interesting way of seeing different parts of the country. Even if you own a cat, it is generally possible to arrange with a friend or neighbour to look after it, to leave them a key, and to give them your phone number at the 'sit' in case anything should arise.

BRIAN MILLS – HOMESITTER

Brian Mills and his wife, who live in Sussex, took up homesitting after he had retired from his job as manager of a poultry farm. As he puts it: 'Having done a seven-day week for most of my life, I had no desire to moon about in a flat for the remainder of it'. Naturally he still has an interest in farming and how it is carried out in different parts of the UK but, as he explains: 'As a general rule you do not go into the farm if there is one that goes with the house. You leave that to the farm manager, and just live in the house and see that everything there is all right. Sometimes there is a bit of relief feeding of livestock at weekends, if this is arranged with the manager, and you will check to see that the water supply is working. If anything is obviously wrong with the stock, or with anything else, you have the manager's telephone number as well as that of the vet'.

He first heard of homesitting about 3 years ago through an enthusiastic letter in *Choice* magazine from a man who was already doing it. He and his wife have been 'sitting' regularly since then, generally in places within a 100-mile radius from their home. He regards it as an opportunity to see nice houses and to enjoy living in other counties – sometimes in fairly isolated villages. Like many flat dwellers not able to keep pets, he enjoys the company of a variety of dogs and cats.

He feels that everyone connected with a 'sit' has to be security-minded regarding the house and its contents, and to be methodical and ready to anticipate anything which may arise.

Before the 'sit' starts, you are furnished with lists of telephone numbers for emergency services – vet, builder, plumber, electrician and usually that of some neighbour who can be called in for advice if the owner cannot be contacted. Also you make sure you start off with a full list of instructions on feeding the pets and on the times of day they are accustomed to being exercised. It has been very rare, in his own experience, to have any occupant of the house around, as children, parents, grandparents will all be away. Occasionally a grown-up son or daughter may call in for some reason, but this is also catered for in advance, so that the sitter knows who they are and what they look like. Sitters are also told about any part-time staff, such as a cleaner or a gardener.

As he points out: 'You treat the house as if it is your own home. My wife and I never leave the house or garden for very long and get in the habit of taking something with us to do so that we can be occupied. If we do have to go out, we try to fit this in with times when the cleaner or gardener is around, or arrange to go out separately'.

Although you need to be alert and methodical, as he explains: 'You quickly get into a routine, and when you are asked back to the same house, it is quite easy to get back into that routine again'.

BERYL ADAMS – CROSSING WARDEN
Beryl Adams enjoys her work as a crossing warden – more popularly known as a 'lollipop lady' – which brings her into contact with parents, children and staff at three junior schools in Uxbridge.

Having worked for years on the buses she is not worried whether the day is wet or fine. 'After all' she says 'If you get soaked, you can soon cycle home and get into a hot bath'.

The school gates open on to a busy road and four times a day she has to be on duty, making sure that the traffic stops for children who must cross in safety. In theory she is on duty for certain set times, but in practice she always stays on to look after the stragglers, who emerge well after the rest of the children have gone. 'It is usually the same ones, week after week' she says. 'They lose their things, or get kept in, and they're always quite a time after the others have left'.

When she took up the work 3 years ago, she applied to the local police station, and found that this can be a long-term job, as lollipop ladies do not retire until 75 or even 80 years of age.

Apart from her traffic duties, she has a husband and grown-up son to look after, as well as running her own home. Mr and Mrs Adams enjoy caravanning and recently toured Scotland. They are looking forward to a holiday in the USA, but this time the caravan will be left behind.

She believes that good health, alertness and a liking for children are needed for her job and, above all, cheerfulness. A big advantage of work related to schools is that the long holidays allow for plenty of travel in the weeks when schools are closed for the vacations.

HAROLD LONGMAN – HOBBYIST

Harold Longman knows a lot about retirement and how to make the most of it. Now 80, he retired from Unilever more than 10 years ago and has been keeping himself occupied and interested ever since. In fact, some of his activities, such as his oil painting, started well before retirement and his home in South Norwood is filled with examples of his talent. He says: 'Plan and have as many hobbies as possible. Take advantage of adult school half-fees for OAPs'. He has certainly done that with his pottery, an art which he took up after retirement. Starting with containers for indoor plants, he quickly progressed to animal and human studies and is at present experimenting with vases using his own technique which gives the effect of tree-bark.

Another idea which he put into practice and recommends to others is: 'Write a book on one's work, trade or subject'. He spent the first year of his retirement writing a book on organisation and methods, his own speciality as Chief Organisation and Methods Officer at Unilever. Since then he has published a volume of poems entitled *Thoughts*. The proceeds of sales from these poems go to cancer research.

He is still a very active man. He and his wife Nina, to whom he has been married for more than 50 years, walk 3 miles a day and, in addition, he has a daily 30-minute workout to keep fit. He advises those who have done little or no exercise before retirement to undertake at least a 3-mile walk or a good swim every day. He believes in eating less but at the same time makes sure of having a good supply of calcium every day, to guard against the tendency of bones to become brittle as people age. He and his wife follow a largely vegetarian diet, with some fish, but they avoid meat, butter and other animal fats.

They are both a picture of health and, right up until he was 80, Mr Longman regularly carried out all the exterior painting at their house. He still does all the interior decoration, as well as the digging of his extensive garden, which is largely given over to vegetables and fruit, and makes them almost self-supporting.

The Longmans take three holidays a year, the longest in winter, plus another in early summer and one in the autumn, and head for warmer places. People still need holidays in retirement, he says, because retirement should not be one long holiday or you become slack and bored. Reading is enjoyable, but should not occupy the whole day or it will soon pall.

'If there is a need to do so', he advises, 'make an income from your hobbies. It could greatly add to your interest in them and their ability to keep you active'. He is in the fortunate position of not needing to increase his income, but he still believes that to fill every day is the most satisfying way of approaching retirement. This does not mean a restless activity to no purpose, but having so many hobbies and interests that the day does not seem to be long enough for everything you wish to do. As he says in one of the poems in his book *Thoughts*: 'The aim is not to retire FROM a thing. But to retire TO something fruitful'.

HAROLD AND JESSIE JUDD – GARDENERS

Retirement and gardens have always gone together, but it is amazing that, in 1984, two top gardening awards were won by retired couples who had left their 60s well behind them.

The first was the award of Gardener of the Year from *Garden News*, given to Harold Judd (81), assisted by his wife, Bessie (80).

The Judd garden in a Dorset village does not contain a lawn, but that is the only thing missing. In this quarter-acre plot there are six different sections, each concentrating on one particular aspect of gardening. There are hundreds of alpines, often planted in old-style solid-stone sinks, bonsai trees which Harold has been growing since 1935 and Lithops (living stone) plants. In addition you can see grape vines, an enormous variety of shrubs and flowers and a very impressive collection of miniature conifers. Another feature is a delightful water garden. Vistas framed by archways can be seen from different parts of the garden, which is opened annually for charity and attracts many visitors from the UK and abroad.

This is by no means the first gardening that Harold Judd has done. Since he was a boy he has tried his hand at growing everything from orange pips to date stones and he won his first prize at a horticultural show when only 10 years old.

Nor has it been easy to keep the gardens that the Judds have created. One in Hertfordshire was devastated by an air raid in World War 2 and, when it had been put to rights, the threat of the M25 motorway overshadowed its future.

Harold Judd retired from work because of ill health when he was 61, but 20 years later he is still going strong. He was 65 when, in 1969, he and his wife moved to Dorset and began work on their new garden which received the *Garden News* award. It took three vans to transfer some 3,000 plants from their previous garden and they joke that the furniture nearly got left behind. At the time, the site was rough heathland, but now it is a beautiful garden with established plants, trees and shrubs set off by mellowed stone.

CHRIS AND LUCY LOFTHOUSE – GARDENERS

The second 'Gardener of the Year' award given by *Garden Answers* went to 80-year-old Chris Lofthouse and his wife Lucy, aged 70. The *Garden Answers* award also shows that there must be some magic in gardening which keeps people young. This was for an all-round garden with fruit and vegetables as well as flowers, shrubs and lawn. In Middleham in the Yorkshire Dales, the Lofthouses have managed to create a superb garden. Yet Lucy is 70 and admits to coming from a rheumaticky family and Chris is 10 years older.

A stream runs through this beautifully-matured garden of two-thirds of an acre and this is criss-crossed by stone bridges and small paths. There is a coppice of yew, birch and copper beech as well as cedar and conifers. Chris Lofthouse is responsible for all tree-pruning and for ditching, and Lucy for mowing.

Summer bedding plants form a colourful border to a rectangular pond and there is an enormous variety of shrubs intermixed with stretches of lawn and venerable apple trees.

Lucy had never had any formal training in gardening, but had taken up the hobby at 12 years of age, when her family had an allotment. Chris comes from a gardening family as both his grandfather and father were professional gardeners. When he and Lucy married 10 years ago, he brought with him all the shrubs from his previous garden, which settled in well in their new location.

The Lofthouses do all their own fencing and walling – in fact there is nothing that they have not tackled in creating this garden, as they have called on no outside assistance.

They are true garden fanatics, whose idea of a perfect summer day is to go out at first light, only coming in for meals and staying out until darkness comes down after 9 o'clock. Apart from its beauty, this is also a very practical garden. At one side of the house are two small greenhouses for raising cuttings and summer bedding plants, and for growing melons, cucumbers and peppers. Beyond these is a vegetable garden, behind a dry stone wall, which provides almost all their needs throughout the year.

One fascinating achievement is their hobby of growing British woodland trees in the form of Japanese miniatures. They say that this is not difficult but these trees must be kept out of doors and not regarded as indoor plants just because of their small size.

REFERENCES

BOOKS

Automobile Association (1984) *Stately Homes, Castles and Gardens in Britain* Automobile Association, Basingstoke.

Beckett, K. (1976) *Plants in Window Boxes* Charles Letts & Co., London.

Benedictus, D. (1976) *Junk* Macmillan, Basingstoke.

Berriedale-Johnson, M. (1985) *Simply Simple Recipes* London Broadcasting Co. Ltd, London.

Boyd, L. (1985) *Window Gardens* Pelham Books, London.

Consumers Association (1978) *Where to Live after Retirement* Consumers Association, London.

Consumers Association (1983) *Approaching Retirement* Consumers Association, London.

Davies, L. (1972) *Easy Cooking for One or Two* Penguin, Harmondsworth, Middlesex.

Gore, I. (1973) *Age and Vitality: Commonsense Ways of Adding Life to Your Years* Unwin, Old Woking, Surrey.

Griffiths, T. (1973) *Enjoy Your Retirement* David & Charles, Newton Abbot.

Harris, H. (1971) *How to Go Collecting Model Soldiers* Patrick Stephens, Wellingborough, Northants.

Humphries, J. (1984) *Part-Time Work* Kogan Page, London.

Ingman, D. (1976) *So You Don't Want to Retire* Arthur Barker, London.

Kannik, P. (19??) *Military Uniforms of the World in Colour* Blandford Press, Poole, Dorset.

Koshak, D. (1978) *Daily Telegraph Guide to Retirement* Collins, London.

Loughton, A. (1976) *Retirement, the New Beginning* Bachman & Turner, London.

Loving, W. (1975) *How to Plan Your Retirement* Woodhead-Faulkner, Cambridge.

Miller, H. (1978) *Countdown to Retirement* Hutchinson Benham Ltd, London.

Patten, M. (1970) *Bedsitter Cookery* Hamlyn, Feltham, Middlesex.

Reader's Digest (1981) *The Easy Path to Gardening* Reader's Digest Association, London.

Rice, P. (1981) *Personal Security* PR Enterprises, Norton Cannon, Herefordshire.

Shortt, J. (1984) *Self-Defence – The Essential Handbook* Sidgwick & Jackson, London.

Wallis, J.H. (1975) *Thinking about Retirement* Pergamon, Oxford.

Whitehorn, Katherine (1981) *Cooking in a Bedsitter* Penguin, Harmondsworth, Middlesex.

GUIDE BOOKS

Blue Guides A. & C. Black, London.

Companion Guides Collins, London.

Travel Guides Berlitz, London.

Visitor's Guides Moorland Publishing Company, Ashbourne, Derbyshire.

PERIODICALS

Weekly

Country Life King's Reach Tower, Stanford Street, London SE1 9LS.

Garden News Peter Law, Park House, 117 Park Road, Peterborough PE1 2TS.

Monthly

Choice Retirement Choice Magazine Company Ltd, 12 Bedford Row, London WC1R 4DU.

Home Overseas 10 East Road, London N1.

Home Security Argosy House, High Street, Orpington, Kent BR6 0LW.

Parkers' Property Price Guide 58 Parker Street, London WC2 5BR.

Period Property Register Chobham Park House, Chobham, Surrey.

Retirement Consort House, 26 Queensway, London W2 3RX.

Yours Help the Aged, St James' Walk, London EC1R 0BE

Bi-Annual

Calendar of Residential Short Courses National Institute of Adult Education (England and Wales), 35 Queen Anne Street, London W1M.

Plain Man's Guide to Air Fares Wakefield Fortune (travel agents), 273 New Cross Road, London SE14.

Overseas Property Guide Thornton Cox Ltd, 3 Colebrook Court, Sloane Avenue, London SW1.

Annual

Agents' Hotel Gazetteer for the Resorts of Europe Hotel Gazetteers, Travel Publications, 30 Grove Road, Beaconsfield, Bucks.

Charities Digest Family Welfare Association, 501 Kingsland Road, London E8.

Floodlight Inner London Education Authority, County Hall, London SE1.

Writers' & Artists' Yearbook A. & C. Black, 35 Bedford Row, London.

Yearbook of Adult Education National Institute of Adult Education, 35 Queen Anne Street, London W1M.

MISCELLANEA

Buyer's Guide to Property Overseas Age Concern/National Housing and Town Planning Council, 60 Pitcairn House, Mitcham, Surrey CR4 3LL.

Buying Property Overseas from publisher of *Homes Overseas*, 10 East Road, London N1.

Caravan & Chalet Site Guide 38 Hampton Road, Teddington, Middlesex.

Food for Thought Health Education Council, 78 New Oxford Street, London WC1.

Guide to the Social Services Macdonald & Evans (Publications) Ltd, Estover Road, Plymouth PL6 7PZ.

Looking after Yourself in Retirement Health Education Council, 78 New Oxford Street, London WC1.

The Property Logbook Davenport Kingdom & Co., Langport, Somerset TA10 9BR.

Protect Your Home H.M.S.O., 49 High Holborn, London WC1.

Someone Like you Can Help London Council of Social Service, 68 Chalton Street, London NW1.

Special Aids to Hearing Royal National Institute for the Deaf, 65 Gower Street, London WC1E 5AH.

Staying Put or Moving On Age Concern/National Housing and Town Planning Council, c/o Age Concern, 60 Pitcairn House, Mitcham, Surrey CR4 3LL.

Your Rights Age Concern, 60 Pitcairn House, Mitcham, Surrey CR4 3LL.

Your Taxes and Savings Age Concern, 60 Pitcairn House, Mitcham, Surrey CR4 3LL.

Voluntary Social Services Directory & Handbook National Council of Social Service, 26 Bedford Square, London WC1.

USEFUL ADDRESSES

THE ABBEYFIELD SOCIETY, 35a High Street, Potters Bar, Hertfordshire.
AGE CONCERN, 60 Pitcairn Road, Mitcham, Surrey CR4 3LL.
AUTOMOBILE ASSOCIATION, Fanum House, Basingstoke, Hants RG21 2EA.
BANK OF ENGLAND, Threadneedle Street, London EC2. (Guide to UK Exchange Control.)
BRITISH ASSOCIATION OF REMOVERS, 279 Grays Inn Road, London WC1.
THE BRITISH ASSOCIATION OF RETIRED PERSONS, 14 Frederick Street, Edinburgh EH2 2HB.
BRITISH EXECUTIVE SERVICE OVERSEAS, 10 Belgrave Square, London SW1.
BRITISH GAS CORPORATION, 152 Grosvenor Road, London SW1.
BRITISH NUTRITION FOUNDATION, 15 Belgrave Square, London SW1.
BRITISH RED CROSS SOCIETY, 9 Grosvenor Crescent, London SW7.
CENTRAL BUREAU FOR EDUCATIONAL VISITS AND EXCHANGES, Seymour Mews House, Seymour Mews, London W1.
CENTRAL COUNCIL FOR THE DISABLED, 34 Eccleston Square, London SW1V 1PE
CITIZENS ADVICE BUREAUX: In most localities. (Enquire at the public library.)
CONSUMERS ASSOCIATION, 14 Buckingham Street, London WC2N 6DS.
COUNSEL & CARE FOR THE ELDERLY, 131 Middlesex Street, London E1.
COUNTRYSIDE COMMISSION, John Dower House, Crescent Place, Cheltenham, Glos, GL50 3RA
CRUSE, 126 Sheen Road, Richmond Road, Surrey TW9 1UR.
DEPARTMENT OF THE ENVIRONMENT, 2 Marsham Street, London SW1.
DEPARTMENT OF HEALTH & SOCIAL SECURITY OVERSEAS GROUP, Newcastle-on-Tyne NE98 1YX. (For local DHSS offices enquire at the public library.)
DISABLED LIVING FOUNDATION, 346 Kensington High Street, London W14 8NS.
DISTRESSED GENTLEFOLKS ASSOCIATION, Vicarage Gate, London W8.
ELECTRICAL ASSOCIATION FOR WOMEN, 25 Fouberts Place, London W1V 2AL.
ELECTRICITY CONSULTATIVE COUNCIL, Great New Street, London EC4.
EMPLOYMENT FELLOWSHIP, Drayton House, Gordon Street, London WC1H 0BE.
FAMILY WELFARE ASSOCIATION, 501 Kingsland Road, London E8.
FRIENDS OF THE ELDERLY, 42 Ebury Street, London SW1W 0LZ.
GREAT BRITAIN CAR CLUB, P.O. Box 11, Romsey, Hants SO5 8XX.
HEALTH EDUCATION COUNCIL, 78 New Oxford Street, London WC1.

OPEN UNIVERSITY, P.O. Box 48, Milton Keynes, Bucks MK7 6AB.

OVERSEAS TERRITORIES INCOME TAX OFFICE, Magdalen House, Trinity Road, Bootle, Merseyside L69 9BB.

PART-TIME CAREERS LTD, 10 Golden Square, London W1.

PHYSICAL EDUCATION ASSOCIATION, 162 Kings Cross Road, London WC1.

PRE-RETIREMENT ASSOCIATION OF GREAT BRITAIN & NORTHERN IRELAND, Greenfield House, 69/73 Manor Road, Wellington, Surrey SM6 0DQ.

PRO DOGS, Rocky Bank, 4 New Road, Ditton, Maidstone, Kent ME20 6AD.

RESEARCH PUBLICATIONS SERVICES LTD, Victoria Hall, Fingal Street, London SE10. (Hobby holidays)

ROTARY INTERNATIONAL IN GREAT BRITAIN AND IRELAND, Sheen Lane House, Sheen Lane, London SW14.

ROYAL AUTOMOBILE CLUB, 149 Pall Mall, London SW1.

ROYAL NATIONAL INSTITUTE FOR THE DEAF, 105 Gower Street, London WC1E 5AH.

ROYAL NATIONAL INSTITUTE FOR THE BLIND, 224 Great Portland Street, London W1.

ROYAL SOCIETY FOR THE PREVENTION OF ACCIDENTS, Cannon House, The Priory, Queensway, Birmingham 4.

ST JOHN AMBULANCE, 1 Grosvenor Crescent, London W1.

SALVATION ARMY, 101 Queen Victoria Street, London EC4.

SAMARITANS, 39 Walbrook, London EC4. (24-hour service)

SOLID FUEL ADVISORY SERVICE, Hobart House, Grosvenor Place, London W1.

SUCCESS AFTER SIXTY (Office Employment) LTD, 40 Old Bond Street, London W1.

TASK FORCE, Clifford House, Edith Villas, London W14.

TOC H, 38 Newark Street, London E1.

UNIVERSAL AUNTS LTD, 250 Kings Road, London SW3. (No upper age limit: employment solely on suitability.)

WOMEN'S INSTITUTES, NATIONAL FEDERATION OF, 39 Eccleston Street, London SW1.

WOMEN'S ROYAL VOLUNTARY SERVICE (WRVS), 17 Old Park Lane, London W1.

A very wide range of help can also be obtained from your local public library, post office and church groups, and from the local newspaper and Yellow Pages classified directory.

INDEX